THE D WORD

12 Steps to Diversity Recovery

Susan McCuistion

The D Word – *12 Steps to Diversity Recovery*

Paperback ISBN: 978-1-953806-41-3
Library of Congress Control Number: 2021909878

Cover Design: Heather Bednorz Design – www.HeatherBednorz.com

Editing: Kimberly Hand – kimmunitee.com

Interior Layout: Amit Dey – amitdey2528@gmail.com

Publisher: Spotlight Publishing™ www.spotlightpublishing.pro

Susan McCuistion
www.susanmccuistion.com

THE D WORD

12 Steps to Diversity Recovery

Susan McCuistion

Goodyear, AZ

Table of Contents

Acknowledgments

"I am surrounded by loving and supportive
family and friends."

This is a mantra I repeat to myself at least once a day, and it's never been truer than this past year—even though the "surrounded" part has mostly been via video calls, text messaging, and social media.

At the beginning and end of this list is my husband of 26 years, Dan. We've been through a lot in those years, and despite it all (or maybe because of it), you remain my rock and my home.

I am grateful to the many mentors, colleagues, and coaches I've had along the way. You've provided the framework for my thinking and the examples for my way of being in this work. You were the sounding boards and the support. I can't list you all because I know I'll forget someone. However, I've tried to express my gratitude along the way. Hopefully, you know who you are, even if we've lost touch. Especially dear to my heart are the Board Members and speakers who believed in the vision of the New Diversity Summit™, even before online conferences were cool.

To my brother, Jeff, "the word man." Thank you for believing in me since the day I was born. Your encouragement and support with every endeavor I've undertaken have meant the world to me.

I've been extremely lucky to have some sister-friends who have seen me through the many different stages in my life. Laura, Peggy, Priya, Maggie, I love you forever!

Finally, to everyone I've coached and trained along the way. I always learn more from you than I think you learn from me. Thank you for sharing your stories with me.

Beginning the Conversation

"Don't tell anyone."

That's what my mom used to say to me, and I never questioned it. I promised never to talk about it.

I knew she was Native American, but I grew up in a White, middle-class neighborhood. All my friends looked just like me, and I never questioned whether I belonged. Then one day, I had a school assignment to write my autobiography. I started with the sentence, "I am Swedish and Native American…"

My dad was able to tell me about the Swedish part. His mother immigrated to the United States when she was three years old. He grew up around her family speaking Swedish and celebrating Swedish traditions. His father's side of the family was primarily of English descent, and they had a family tree that went back to the original colonists in the United States.

When I asked my mom about the Native American part, she wouldn't talk about it. Instead, my dad took me over to the bookshelves, and he pulled out a book I had seen a million times before. My mom's birth certificate was in the book. My dad took it out, and he pointed to the line that said "Race." He looked at me and repeated, "You're half. You're half."

"Half what?!" I asked in a defiant 12-year-old way.

I looked to where he was pointing, and on the line next to "Race" on my mother's birth certificate was typed the word "Red."

At that moment, a flood of questions filled my head. What did it mean to be "Red"? Worse yet, what did it mean to be half of something? Did I really belong? Could my friends still be my friends?

I knew I could no longer *not* talk about it. In fact, it felt like not talking about it was creating more problems than it solved.

This "not talking about it" thing was true in my childhood, and it's true in your communities and organizations. How many of your friends and co-workers are not talking about it and hiding parts of who they are because they're afraid or even ashamed? How many are not talking about it because they look or believe differently than others in your circle? How many of *you* are not talking about it because to do so might mean you're not politically correct and may say something that could cost you your job?

Diversity & Inclusion (D&I) programs have been around for years, but we still don't get it. We continue to see an abundance of diversity issues within organizations and society at large. There is a lack of women and Black, Indigenous, People of Color (BIPOC) in leadership roles within organizations. Older generations berate Millennial and Gen Z employees for being job-hoppers and not loyal to the company. We punish employees for not being politically correct instead of educating or trying to understand different perspectives. Situations arise on a regular basis that create a social media nightmare for organizations resulting in public shaming and forced apologies.

It's no different outside of work. The COVID-19 pandemic has brought to light many long-standing systemic inequities based on race/ethnicity, gender, and socioeconomic status. Anti-Asian hate crimes increased 150% in 2020.[1] The confluence of the pandemic and the killing of George Floyd brought the Black Lives Matter movement and global protests to the forefront. More attention has been paid to issues within Indigenous communities, where American Indian and Alaska Native (AI/AN) women are murdered at a rate of more than ten times the national average.[2] Low-wage workers are most often in jobs deemed essential, with no option for remote work, and are more susceptible to exposure to the COVID-19 virus.[3] In December 2020, women accounted for all 140,000 jobs lost in the United States.[4]

And now, cancel culture. People are being called out and shamed for things they said 20 or more years ago. We force people into fixtures of their past and assume they haven't grown or changed in years. Who hasn't said or done anything foolish at some point in their lives? I know I certainly have!

The irony of this work is that we teach tolerance, but there's a place where we need to become intolerant of behavior that harms our fellow human beings. People can believe whatever they want, but when they take action to impose those beliefs upon others or demand that "you must believe as I do," they've crossed a line. When people act in ways that discriminate against others because of who they are, they've crossed a line. I don't care where you lie on the political continuum, the color of your skin, your ethnicity, your gender identity or expression, your age, your sexual orientation, or anything else you use to identify yourself by—there are people across all spectrums who demand "they" believe and behave like "us." Not only have we lost track of how to treat each other with respect, but we've also lost the ability to have conversations that lead to understanding each other as human beings.

I've heard the same excuses for 20 years, and I can only come to one conclusion—our approach to Diversity and Inclusion (D&I) is broken. In fact, I find many people still don't know exactly what D&I is. There's a false belief that it's counts and numbers or meeting quotas. Myths about the necessity of hiring less-qualified candidates and reverse discrimination continue, and the way we handle D&I issues when they arise only serve to perpetuate these myths.

D&I has become a game of optics.

I learned this lesson very early on in this work. My opening story is one I've told for as long as I've been in this field, because I was told, "Susan, you have to get out there as soon as possible that you're Native American, because White people have no credibility in this work." In an effort to create credibility within the field and give an appearance of BIPOC in leadership, Chief Diversity Officer and other diversity roles are created within organizations and populated with BIPOC employees. Some of these employees know they are in the role simply because it looks good for the company. Many of them are well qualified for other leadership positions within the company, but they are stuck in their diversity roles because of the optics. As a result, organizations overcorrect based on color optics and underrepresent other types of diversity like ability, generation, sexual orientation, veteran status, etc. Additionally, White culture is wholly dismissed[5] as if "diversity" is reserved only for those not from the majority population. If the end result is equity for all, I would expect equitable representation of all types of diversity, *especially* within the D&I field. Unfortunately, that's not the case.

Change doesn't happen overnight; what I've witnessed in over 20 years of doing this work is organizations seem to think closing business for a day of unconscious bias training will fix all their woes. Better yet, they can save time if it's only a 2-hour workshop. They want all the applause for paying attention to diversity for a day and none of the criticism for not taking the time to embed it into their day-to-day systems.

I have never been a fan of "doing diversity because it's the right thing to do." I don't like diversity as optics or diversity for publicity. However, I guarantee you I can find a D&I link to every challenge we have as human beings because, in the end, our challenges are about our different perspectives of the world, which are formed as a result of our diversity.

I'm a mathematician by education, so I'm good at finding patterns and creating meaning out of those patterns. I consider myself a diversity generalist and meta-diversity professional. Many people are great at specific topics within D&I–gender, age, race/ethnicity, socioeconomic status. I bring together my experience and knowledge in the field of D&I with the research of related topics outside the field to create connections and new insights. If you want information about the fields outside of D&I that I've connected within this book, you can visit the work of the experts in those fields. If you want to learn more about vulnerability, listen to Brené Brown. Emotional Intelligence? Daniel Goleman. Compassion? Read The Dalai Lama. What I have done is brought their ideas to the field of D&I. You'll see a different spin here.

I always try to see things from different perspectives. A dear friend once said to me, "Susan, you are at the same time the easiest and the most difficult person to talk to. Easy, because I can say anything to you. Difficult, because you'll always give me another way to think about it." I pride myself on this. Yes, it can be frustrating for people who don't understand me. However, I value different perspectives, and there is always more than one way to think about a situation. That doesn't necessarily mean every way is right or wrong, but there's always more than one way, and sometimes, there is a lot of gray.

To be clear, I'm not talking about extremes here, nor am I talking about giving anyone a "pass" for bad behavior. We all must be held accountable for our actions. However, we must meet people where they are. I have friends who can be quite polarized and see actions or events as simply "right" or "wrong." The best we might be able to do is create a foundational understanding of "We're all human." The truth is, not everyone is ready to hear about topics like systemic racism and privilege. They're just not. The "what-about-ism" that follows is not worth the argument. If they're ready to hear more, we'll talk. If not, frankly, I'm not going to spend my energy trying to convince them otherwise, nor is it worth sacrificing our relationship.

My business coach said to me, "You say you want compassion, but every time I talk to you, you're mad."

My response? "I believe in love. I just want everyone to get along. And yeah, it makes me mad we can't. That we're running around yelling, pointing fingers and arguing instead of listening. Everyone. Majority folks. Non-majority folks. Colleagues who teach this stuff. I know one Chief Diversity Officer who prides herself on yelling at people when they are doing something that offends her or that she thinks might offend other people. I've had colleagues tell me they've been at the end of that from other 'leaders' in this space, and I have, too. If we can't set the example and direction for how we want things to be, then we shouldn't be doing this work."

Upon reflection of my response, I realized—we are addicted to D&I as it is.

Science shows we are addicted to our emotions. Our bodies react with a flood of hormones and chemicals based on what we are feeling, and we get addicted to them. Strong feelings release adrenaline, and our bodies get addicted to the rush, so we find more and more ways to get that rush. When we get angry and fight against things, we get that rush. When we get indignant about the way things are, we get that rush. When we yell and take up arms, it invokes our fight or flight response, which turns on the adrenaline, and we get that rush.

The definition of insanity is to do the same thing over and over again and expect different results. Yet, we do the same things repeatedly with diversity and inclusion, somehow expecting turnover will get better, or we're going to attract better talent, or people will be treated more equitably and systemic injustices will magically be rectified. We wring our hands and lament when training doesn't work, but we don't do anything differently. Instead, we keep pushing the same party lines, becoming indignant, frustrated, and angry.

We are addicted to the adrenaline rush which comes when things don't improve.

As long as we remain addicted to the lack of equitable outcomes, we will not solve anything. We spend so much time *fighting against* things like hate and discrimination and inequality. What if we could refocus and *stand for* things like love and fairness and equity? (I've been talking about this for years—it's even been modified and spoken about by others who have heard it, and it will be addressed further in Step 5.)

In the end, I really am a Pollyanna. I want a peaceful world where everyone is respected, and everyone gets along. Call it privilege. Call it fragility. Call it being a Next Generation Flower Child. Whatever.

The truth is, we won't have a peaceful world where everyone gets along *until* everyone is respected. *Until* we can understand that right now, everyone is *not* treated with equity. *Until* we fix systemic issues and all the –isms and phobias. *Until* we love each other as human beings and understand we are all connected. Until these are fixed, *everyone* is held back.

In this book, I offer you my piece of the puzzle to bringing a more humanitarian approach to D&I. I hope you find it helpful.

Navigating This Book

Each chapter is devoted to one of The 12 Steps to Diversity Recovery™. You'll read about the main issues within each step, and you'll also see some Diversity Tough Love™ connected to each step. Diversity Tough Love™ is intended to bring to light some of the long-lived myths around D&I work.

There are exercises at the end of each chapter that will help you practice the lessons of that chapter. I've also set up a free online portal for readers of this book which contains more exercises and references for each step. You can sign up for the portal at www.TheDWordDiversity.com.

Finally, I invite you to take a minute to watch this welcome video, where you can learn a little more about me and my work.

Scan the QR Code with your smartphone to watch the video.

The 12 Steps to Diversity Recovery™

Step 1: We acknowledge that separating people into groups of "us" and "them" is not only physically, mentally, emotionally, and spiritually harmful for everyone, it also is detrimental to our personal relationships.

Step 2: We recognize we are all connected and a part of the social systems which weave through our societies, nations, and world. We are all human; we share basic human needs for belonging. We are also all different; therefore, we are all diverse.

Step 3: We acknowledge we have much in common, and we share values. We allow ourselves to see differences, and we discover there are different ways to express our shared values.

Step 4: We accept we cannot resolve our differences by pointing fingers and placing blame. We are committed to learning how to have conversations about our differences.

Step 5: We discover when we can achieve fair outcomes, everyone benefits. We release notions of equality and act with equity.

Step 6: We work to build a better understanding of ourselves, because knowing who we are is key to understanding each other.

Step 7: We discover we can remain true to ourselves while allowing others the space to be true to themselves.

Step 8: We cultivate the humility to admit we don't know all the answers and to ask the questions we need to ask in order to learn.

Step 9: We maintain nonjudgment and curiosity when we see someone behave differently in word, action, or deed.

Step 10: We notice when we feel good, we are in alignment with our beliefs, values and expectations. When we don't feel good, we aren't in alignment.

Step 11: We remember learning about ourselves and others often happens through making mistakes. We grant ourselves, and others, grace when we mess up.

Step 12: We know learning is a lifelong journey. We commit to taking the necessary time to build better connections in all our relationships.

Download your copy here: http://bit.ly/12StepsDownload

Us vs. Them

Step 1:

We acknowledge that separating people into groups of "us" and "them" is not only physically, mentally, emotionally, and spiritually harmful for everyone, it also is detrimental to our personal relationships.

Let's face it—we live in a very polarized society. Every day, we hear scary stories about the spread of disease and how diagnoses are mishandled. We're told about tension in our government and accusations of abuse of power. We see talking heads spewing emotional arguments without always having the facts. We spend a lot of time arguing and pointing fingers to blame others for what's going wrong. We perpetuate stereotypes and tend to believe that there's one correct answer for everything.

It seems the collective mindset is, "If I'm right, then you're wrong."

From the day we are born, we receive messages from our parents, teachers, and communities about what is right and what is wrong. We learn these patterns and behaviors through direct instruction, trial and error, or simple observation. We are taught how to behave, although those teaching us don't often take the time to explain to us *why* we're doing what we're doing. For instance, many in the United States were raised with parents who said, "What's the magic word?" when we asked for something. If you were brought up this way, you know the magic word is "Please." We usually figure out that saying "Please" and "Thank you" is tied to the value of "politeness." When we encounter someone who wasn't taught to say "Please" and "Thank you," we think they're rude.

At some point, what we're taught becomes ingrained. We *know* being polite means saying "Please" and "Thank you." We *know* the right way to show respect is to say, "Yes, Sir," or "Yes, Ma'am."

We think we know what is right or wrong, but we don't understand *why* we were taught certain behaviors are "right" or "wrong." We especially don't understand when someone gets offended by something we think is "right" or take the time to consider why they might think it's "wrong." It's easy to believe our way is the right way, but other people, who may do things quite differently than we do, believe their way is the right way, too. As a result, we get stuck in a loop of "either/or" thinking—either I'm right, or you are. We fail to consider that two seemingly opposite things can actually both be true.

The core beliefs behind either/or thinking stem from fear. Changing our foundational beliefs, accepting there may be beliefs different from our own, or, heaven forbid, admitting we might be wrong can be fearful. If we see things from a different perspective, are we still living our values? Are we being authentic? Self-doubt and fear of being wrong trigger our egos. After all, if we are wrong, people might think we're stupid or ignorant—and who wants to be either?

Instead of trying to understand others, we get entrenched in our own positions and fight back. Rather than trying to discover our common humanity, we engage in actions that perpetuate –isms and phobias.

Human beings are tribal. We are more comfortable around people who look and act like us. When we encounter differences, we fight against our brain's natural tendency to defend against them. We experience fear of "others" because we lack experience with them. Widening our circle to include people who may be quite different from us takes a conscious effort, which can make many of us feel uncomfortable.

One of the roots of us/them thinking stems from our natural desire to belong to a group.[1] If I am confronted in ways that challenge my group's thinking, I can either: 1) defend my thoughts and actions; or 2) change my thoughts and actions and risk being kicked out of my group. In addition to the internal threat our brain triggers based on our new experience, we now have an external threat to manage—the group resistance. Our desire to be part of a group is so great that researchers have found[2] the brain processes exclusion as physical pain. When we are rejected socially, our brains release the same opioids into our systems that are released when we experience physical pain. These natural pain killers help ease the mental and emotional pain we feel from these dismissals.

Stress has a biological purpose in our lives, and we will never escape it. However, too many of us live with too much negative stress in our lives. In fact, our brains have a "negativity bias"[3]—they are more attuned and react more strongly to unpleasant news. From an evolutionary perspective, this makes sense. However, responding to the threats in our modern world—many of which are invented and not real—can leave us exhausted, stressed, and irritable.

The sad part is that politicians, advertisers, and others have learned to use this negativity bias against us. They feed us with fears of "strangers" and "what if" based on nothing more than images in our minds. Many of our fears are imagined.

Fear and distrust are not only inhibitors to creating relationships; they are also bad for our health. People who harbor a general distrust of others are at a "greater risk of dementia compared to those who were more trusting, even after accounting for other risk factors like age, sex, certain heart health markers, smoking status, and more."[4] They are also more likely to have heart disease. People who are hostile towards others have a higher risk for stroke than friendly people.

Real or not, our brains and bodies still react to these events the same way. We go into fight or flight. Cortisol, adrenaline, and a flood of other harmful hormones and chemicals are released into our system.[5] When we can't release the stress, the effects of it live on in our bodies.

We are not fundamentally good at understanding differences. We rarely take time to explore how we formed our own views or ask ourselves why we feel the way we do about certain topics. When confronted with conflicting beliefs, it's much simpler to divide ideas into "right" and "wrong" than to understand the complex nuances that form our beliefs, values, and behaviors in our complicated world.

What's The "D" Word Got to Do With It?

When we hear the word "diversity," we tend to go outward. We think about how people are "different from me." Diversity is about "them."

We travel to a foreign country, and we want to learn all about *them*. What should I do to get along with *them*? Do I kiss, bow, or shake hands when I greet *them*? How should I address *them*? We want to learn all the do's and don'ts to avoid embarrassing ourselves and others.

In business, we want to understand how to recruit or retain or engage a particular group, so we try to understand what motivates women or African Americans or Millennials. We want to build our market share in a distinct segment, so we spend millions of dollars researching that segment. We want to set up business in a different country, so we learn the necessary laws to keep us out of trouble and develop the essential relationships to facilitate our new venture.

Focusing on "them," whether in personal or business situations, creates a dichotomy. It sets up in-groups and out-groups, which only continue to divide us. We judge our own behaviors as "right," while behaviors that are different from ours are "wrong." Even if we can withhold our judgment, we think different styles and practices are out of the norm when they're just out of *our* norm.

Worse, when we think diversity is about "them," we opt ourselves out of the equation. We don't stop to think about the perspective we bring to situations or how others might be viewing us.

Indeed, understanding "them" and wanting to learn about "them" is helpful, but "they" are not all we need to know. When we only take time to understand "them," we get a partial picture of the situation, and we stay stuck in our own perspective.

Diversity Tough Love:

It's essential to understand ourselves first before we jump into trying to understand others.

The Price of Hate and Disconnection

I am an eternal optimist. I believe people are basically good. I believe 99% of us wake up in the morning with good intentions—to go to work, make a decent living, take care of our families, connect with our friends, and help our communities. I don't believe we wake up intentionally trying to hurt others, but, inevitably, we do. Why? Because we only see our own perspectives and don't understand how our views exclude others.

Never is that more evident than it is right now. At every turn, there's news about people being mistreated, excluded, and harmed, and social and political turmoil often seems impossible to escape. It leaves us feeling stressed out in almost every aspect of our lives, and we carry that stress with us into work every day. The mental, emotional, and physical toll this turmoil takes impacts us all, regardless of our role—victim, perpetrator, or observer.

It's essential to look at all three groups because we can't solve hate and discrimination issues unless we understand them from a holistic perspective. *We are all part of the system, and we're all connected. What affects one person or group of people affects us all.* (More about this in Step 2.)

Naturally, when we think about acts of hate and discrimination, our thoughts instantly go to the victims targeted in these acts. Our human instinct to ease and soothe their pain kicks into gear, and we want to jump in to fix the immediate situation. However, the detrimental effects of such acts linger long beyond the initial furor.

Victims of discrimination are subject to increased rates of depression, hypertension, certain cancers, and a host of other illnesses and diseases.[6] Even "perceived discrimination" was associated with increased mortality in older adults, and merely being a racial minority can lead to greater levels of stress. A reported 18.2% of Blacks, compared to 3.5% of Whites, experienced emotional stress, and 9.5% of Blacks, compared to 1.6% of Whites, experienced physical stress.[7]

The devastating effects of these acts aren't limited to just Black, Indigenous, and People of Color (BIPOC) or other underrepresented groups. They extend to majority Whites, as well. In United States counties where Whites expressed more implicit and explicit bias, both Blacks and Whites showed increased death rates from circulatory diseases.[8] In communities where high levels of bias exist, people are less likely to trust and bond with each other, leading to a lack of social connectedness. This lack of connection is more detrimental to our health than obesity, smoking, and high blood pressure.[9]

People who engage in racist, sexist, or homophobic behavior experience a potent mix of negative emotions—such as fear and guilt—when their behavior is brought to their attention. These emotions may block their ability to develop further awareness and, instead, lead to avoidance and defensiveness.[10] As a result, it becomes easier for perpetrators to dehumanize others, further justifying oppressive and inhuman behaviors. Such justification diminishes compassion and can rip an individual's moral and spiritual fiber in two.

Diversity Tough Love:

Learning about diversity & inclusion (and related issues)
is a developmental process.
Some topics are suitable for beginners; other topics take more
expertise to tackle.

Finally, observing these events doesn't protect us from the emotional, physical, and mental consequences.

Merely watching an event triggers a special class of neurons in our brain to engage. Mirror neurons are brain cells that fire not only when we do something but also when we observe someone else do the same thing.[11] Have you ever cringed when you saw someone else stub their toe? Those are the mirror neurons in action, reminding you of the pain you felt when you stubbed your toe. These same mirror neurons fire when we witness traumatic events—like someone being beaten or abused. The neurons fire, and our brain reacts as if we're being beaten. Cortisol, adrenaline, and a flood of other potentially harmful hormones and chemicals get released into our system.[12] The result is not only empathy for the other person but also added stress on our bodies.

Completing Step 1:
Understanding Your Perspective

Us/them thinking is how human beings are built for survival. Overcoming our natural human preference for it requires us to be ever mindful of it, as it is not something we can outgrow. However, moving beyond us/them is necessary for our health, the continued success of our relationships, and ultimately, building a fair and equitable society for everyone. Below are a few suggestions to start shifting this mindset.

Think about a person you're close to—a brother or sister, a best friend, a spouse. Do you see the world in *precisely the same way* they do? Absolutely not. There are probably plenty of times when you've disagreed on a topic, and these are people with whom you probably have a lot in common.

Now, think about how little you know about someone you've just met. Why would you expect them to act and think the way you do when even your closest loved ones don't?

We don't often stop to reflect and determine how we formed our views and who or what influenced us. And yet, we filter our judgments and assumptions based on these very views. Until we fully grasp our own perspective, it isn't easy to step into another's shoes and truly understand their perspective.

Below are ideas for looking inward to better understand your worldview and overcome us/them thinking:

- Journal about your life story. Who influenced you the most? What events shaped you? Where did you cultivate your most deeply held beliefs?

- What are your top three values? How do you express these values through your behavior towards others?

- Try a little "we all" thinking: The next time you have an us/them disagreement with someone, instead of driving home your counterpoint, find a common value on which to agree. For instance, suppose someone says, "Those people just don't know how to act!" Rather than arguing about where they grew up and why their behavior might be different, your response could be, "Can we agree that everyone wants to be respected?" Accept that the only resolution you have might be the things you have in common.

Focusing on the things we have in common is usually more difficult than it sounds, especially in the heat of a disagreement; however, "we all" can go a long way to diffusing "us/them." (We'll discuss more about having conversations in Step 4.)

(I have a free online portal for book readers at www.TheDWordDiversity.com, where you can access more exercises and resources for this and subsequent steps.)

We Are All Connected

Step 2:

We recognize we are all connected and part of the social systems which weave through our societies, nations, and world. We are all human; we share basic human needs for belonging. We are also all different; therefore, we are all diverse.

The Six Degrees of Separation theory claims every person in the world can be connected to any other person through only five other people.[1] Some have criticized the initial experiment, retested it, and found it correct. Since the advent of social media, degrees of connection appear to have shrunk from six to four.[2] Think of it— just three people between you and anyone else in the world. It seems impossible.

If the COVID-19 pandemic of 2020-21 has taught us anything, it's that we live in a hyper-connected world. One event can steer us in an entirely different direction—from causing companies to quickly adjust to work-from-home plans, which they resisted for years, to a well-deserved and prolonged focus on social justice issues.

Connection and Belonging

Building connection is one of our most basic human needs, and we are socially connected now more than ever.[3] Positive social connections are good for our health and may increase our lifespan.[4] Our brains are wired to help the people we're connected with, which helps us build resilience and reduce stress.[5] Our connections also help us:

- Build self-awareness. We learn our values, connect to our beliefs, and deepen our self-understanding. We gain a sense of what motivates us, which gives us a stronger sense of purpose.

- Discover and explore new perspectives. We learn that there is not just one "right" and one "wrong" way for every situation. Embracing different perspectives helps open our minds to other possibilities and build our problem-solving skills. We learn two answers can both be right at the same time.

- Build empathy and understanding. The more we understand ourselves and others, the better we can create more profound and meaningful relationships. We can help other people in more authentic ways—and the benefits of our connection perpetuate.

"Connectedness" and "belonging" are often linked. Belonging is the extent to which we feel accepted by the groups we are connected to. For example, I am connected to my community because I own a home there; however, I don't necessarily feel like I belong because I'm not active in community groups and have little knowledge of local events. We can feel connected to our work because we like our day-to-day tasks, yet we can still feel like we don't belong if we think we're not heard or valued. While it may be relatively easy to find points of connection with others, feeling as if we belong may be more elusive.

Feeling a sense of belonging is key to moving beyond the "D" word and building more inclusive workplaces and communities. "Employees who feel a strong sense of belonging, compared to employees with a low sense of belonging, demonstrate a 50% reduction in turnover risk, a 56% increase in performance, and a 75% decrease in employee sick days."[6]

Cultivating compassion is just one skill that can help us nurture more connected communities and workplaces. On the surface, compassion sounds like a soft skill. However, compassion isn't just about being kind to other people and doing nice things for them. Instead, it's an active process through which we build skills and knowledge to understand what kind of help is wanted, rather than assuming what is needed. We'll see how compassion can further build connection and inclusion as we work through The 12 Steps to Diversity Recovery™.

We Are All Human—and We Are All Different

We are all human, and we deserve to be safe.

We are all human, and we deserve to be respected.

We are all human, and we deserve to be loved.

It's important to focus on the essential humanity of us all. However, we are not all the same. We have different life experiences, which create different perspectives. We have talents and different gifts. No two people are the same.

While we are all human, to fully understand each other, we must also grasp that we are all different.

The previous statement may seem obvious, yet as we move through our busy days, do we truly live by it?

In the United States, I've seen signs and slogans suggesting "diversity" is about eliminating the White race. Of course, that's nonsense. But the overwhelming impression is that diversity means "not White." I coach White folks all the time who think they aren't diverse. They think they don't have a culture. And part of what's perpetuating this idea is that we use "diversity" as a code word.

What does that mean? We're afraid to talk about differences, so instead of saying "race" or "gender" or "age" or any other specific factor, we say "diverse." We say we want more "diverse" candidates for our jobs. We say we want "diverse" hires. We talk about promoting "diversity." When we use the word "diversity" in this way, we are using it as a code word to mean non-majority people[1].

"Diverse" becomes anyone different from the norm. And who's the standard? In the United States, it's White, heterosexual, Christian men. Anyone who is not that is considered "diverse." Identifying diversity in this way becomes problematic because it automatically excludes all White, heterosexual, Christian men from *their* diversity. Because they are considered "not diverse," they have no stake in promoting diversity. In fact, in some cases, "diversity" becomes an issue for them to fight against. The irony of using "diversity" as a code word is that we create in-groups and out-groups—the exact thing we want to avoid.

Some of the issues we encounter around diversity can be unpleasant or make us feel uncomfortable. We might not believe we have the skills to address these issues directly, or we're worried about offending people. We don't like that everyone isn't treated equally, but we're concerned that we will seem to be playing favorites if we don't treat everyone the same. Rather than dealing with uncomfortable diversity issues, we put them off or avoid them altogether, hoping they'll simply go away.

Diversity is. There is no way to avoid it. The world's population is diverse, so the talent pool is diverse, so our organizations are diverse. Our communities are diverse, so our schools and our places of worship are

---

[1] *"Majority" looks different depending on where we are in the world. From my perspective in the United States, the "majority" is White, heterosexual, Christian, and male. If you're reading this somewhere else in the world, insert whoever your majority is. NOTE: The majority isn't necessarily the group with the numbers—it's the group with the power (i.e., the group that gets to write the rules of society). So, while one group may be larger, another group may have the power and thus be the majority.*

diverse. Diversity is simply the variety of perspectives and experiences that make up the human population. Pick out any two people. You now have diversity.

Diversity Tough Love:

We are all diverse.

There have been heads of diversity within organizations forced to apologize and fired for speaking this truth.[7] Diversity isn't just skin deep. What you see on the outside is not who a person is on the inside. Someone may look like they belong to the majority but may have an abilities gap or come from a different socio-economic background. Someone from a particular race or ethnicity may significantly differ from others of the same race or ethnicity.

Misconceptions about diversity operate at all levels of society, but let's focus on workplace implications.

Organizations often "do diversity" because it's the "right" thing. The truth is, it's the only thing. When we look at diversity broadly—the influences, experiences, and education that create our unique perspectives in the world—it becomes evident that diversity is a part of every interaction we have. It's how we see the world—and how we interpret what we are seeing.

If diversity is the world's "default" state, why do organizations need to pay attention to it? To ensure inclusion. Inclusion is the first step to belonging, and belonging results in more successful businesses.

While we are all diverse, we are not necessarily all included—nor does everyone feel they belong. Systemic issues exist, and not everyone has equal opportunity. Women, BIPOC populations, Lesbian/Gay/Bisexual/ Transgender people, those who are differently-abled, and others have been excluded from organizations and leadership because they don't look, act, or think like the majority population. However, the solution does not mean blindly putting someone into a job to check off a box or fill a quota. Companies using this approach are doing it all wrong. The point is to make sure you have the most qualified person in a job regardless of gender, race, or other difference. By limiting your selection to only people who look, work, or act like you, you may have missed the most qualified person for the job.

The sad reality is that it's easier to go along with the status quo than make the changes necessary to build belonging in our organizations through inclusive policies and practices. It's easy for financially successful companies to overlook diversity, inclusion, and belonging *simply because they are successful.* However, are they sustainable? Will their organizational knowledge pass from generation to generation if one is not valued? Will they be able to innovate and maintain a customer base in our hyper-connected and diverse world?

When we fail to acknowledge diversity in our organizations, we cannot effectively recruit, retain, or promote employees; we do not understand our customers or constituents; we lose productivity and innovation. By paying attention to diversity within organizations, we admit we are aware of inequities and acknowledge that we will do something about them.

Inclusion requires us to stop using "diversity" as a code word for "different" and get comfortable having actual conversations about differences. If you're having trouble recruiting African American candidates, then say it. If you're having trouble retaining Latino employees, then say it. If you're noticing that women aren't making it past middle management, then say it. And, if your annual engagement survey shows that White men are less engaged than any other group, say that, too.

When we stop using euphemisms and code words, we can get specific about our challenges and solutions and ensure we have the best talent to run our organizations.

Recognizing diversity means we may need to change where and how we recruit. We may need to adjust our ideas about what "good leadership" looks like and accept that there are many different (and equally effective) ways to lead. We may need to learn more about how others see us, not just how we see others. Recognizing diversity means being aware, keeping an open mind, and admitting that our way is not the only way to see the world.

Diversity is our world's natural, default state and the basis for small- and large-scale person-to-person interaction. Organizations that recognize this, plan for it, and engage with it will be more prepared to meet the demands of the future workforce than those who do not.

Inclusion and belonging may be optional, but diversity just is.

How you deal with it is up to you.

Completing Step 2:
Explore Connections and Get Clear about "Diversity"

We are taught, "We're all human," and, in many cases, we're also taught that noticing and talking about differences is not "polite." It is essential to understand our common humanity and appreciate our differences in order to benefit from more meaningful connections. (Find more exercises and resources at the online portal: www.TheDWordDiversity.com.)

Here are three tips for exploring connection and getting clear about "diversity":

- Play "Six Degrees of Separation." Pick a person—CEO in an organization, celebrity, or someone you admire—and see if you can figure out how many connections it would take to get an introduction to them. (If you'd like to experiment with connections to me, I'd love to meet you!)

- Watch your language. How do you use the word "diverse," and what do you *really* mean? Do you use it in a way that's "politically correct" so as not to offend? Consider this: Not saying exactly what you mean lends itself to confusion and could be construed as offensive.

- Look for ways in which those you may not think of as "diverse" are, in fact, diverse. Don't assume you know everything about a person based on their looks. (If you think you don't do that, think again!)

There Are Many Ways to Be Right

Step 3:

We acknowledge we have much in common, and we share values.
We allow ourselves to see differences, and we discover there are
different ways to express our shared values.

A manager once told me she had learned a big lesson—she was a direct communicator, and she always assumed everyone would come to her to discuss issues directly. After all, she was open and regularly invited people to let her know if they had any questions.

She noticed that one of her employees had become a little bit distant and didn't seem to be speaking to her. She called the employee into her office and found out that the employee had expectations that were the complete opposite. Her employee had expected *her* to approach them rather than the other way around directly. Both the manager and the employee wanted the project to be successful, but their two approaches were at odds. They both had assumed the other should just know their preferred approach.

Unless we stop to think about it, it's easy to go through life believing, "Everyone else is just like me, and we were all taught the same things"—except we aren't.

The Many Faces of Respect

One of the most common discussions in seminars I facilitate centers around the idea that everyone wants to be respected. I've discovered that we don't *truly* respect other people, despite our best intentions.

Why?

We're taught to believe, "We're all human," which assumes we all have the same fundamental experience of the world. We judge others' behavior based on what we were taught was "respectful" and "disrespectful" behavior. When we treat people like we want to be treated, we're assuming they have the same definition of "respect" that we do—but they don't. Consider:

- Direct eye contact is respectful behavior. So is lack of eye contact.
- Saying "yes ma'am" to a woman in the Southern United States is respectful. Doing the same to a woman in the Midwest is disrespectful.
- Speaking directly to a person with whom you have a conflict is considered "professional," and that is "respectful." Yet, indirect communicators might view direct communication as "rude" and "disrespectful."

Nearly every organization has "respect" as a fundamental value. The intent is good. However, values around respect are typically written assuming we all know what respect is. Specific behavior is rarely described, leaving far too much open to interpretation, leading to misunderstanding. For example:

- "We treat one another with respect and take pride in the significant contributions that come from the diversity of individuals and ideas."

- "We depend on the relationships we have and respect each other and those we work with."

- "Respect helps us to value differences, to appreciate each person for her or his unique qualities. Through respect, we help bring out the full potential of each person."

Of course, we all want to be treated with respect. We all try to be respectful to others. But what does "respectful behavior" look like, and exactly how does respect help us value differences?

To be truly respectful, we must first understand that there is a wide range of behaviors that are considered respectful. Then, we must develop the skills necessary to discern which behavior is appropriate for the current situation. Simply treating other people like you want to be treated isn't enough. What if they don't want to be treated like you want to be treated?

Diversity Tough Love:

Treating people the way you want to be treated isn't always the best course of action.

We can value our common humanity *and* begin to understand that there may be more than one right answer or one right way to do things. The world isn't necessarily either/or. It can be both/and. When we think from both/and, we understand different perspectives, even though they may be contrary to our own. We can admit that we don't have all the answers and engage in conversations to learn rather than to win.

Get over it—you're biased!

One of the concepts people are most resistant to in diversity and inclusion is the idea of bias. It's typically thrown about as an insult, and we think of it as a negative thing. We all want to believe we aren't biased, but the reality is, *we are all biased.* It's how our brains work.

Diversity Tough Love:

We can't get rid of bias.

The human brain gets bombarded with 11 million bits of information per second, but it can only process about fifty[1]. It compares data in every second to data collected in the past as a way to filter out unimportant information quickly. Bias is simply a preference for information we already know.

We can't fix bias or get rid of it, but it's not the bias that matters. Bias just makes us human. It's what we *do* with our biases that can positively or negatively impact our businesses and our lives.

We begin forming our biases even before we're born. We learn to like the type of food our mothers eat; we learn to prefer the language our mothers speak. Through chemical reactions in our mothers' bodies, we discover what makes our mothers happy or fearful, and we react in the same way. The pathways carved into our brains form our early perspectives and preferences.

As we grow up and go to school, what we learn and how we learn it inform our growing perspectives and preferences. The books we use, the emphasis of our teachers, and other influences all feed into and reinforce our views. By the time we're seven years old, most of our beliefs and behaviors have been formed by listening to and observing the people around us, and we develop a sense of what is "normal." Ninety-five percent of our actions are subconscious.[2]

That number may sound impossible but think about your typical day. You wake up to an alarm clock, and you either jump out of bed right away, or you hit the snooze button. (Those of you who are snooze button people, you know exactly how many times you can hit that button before you *really* have to get out of bed!) You wander to the coffee pot or into the shower. You follow the same routines, and perhaps the first actual decision you make is what to wear—if you hadn't laid it out the night before.

We move through our days mostly on automatic pilot, so it's only natural to *not* think about how other people might be different—until we get shocked out of our stupor by something unexpected they say or do.

We can break this cycle and mitigate bias by seeking new experiences and learning new things, which helps us create new perspectives. With these new perspectives, we see events differently and create new meaning in our world.

Right versus wrong

Diversity Tough Love:
There is more than one way to be right.

Some things are always right. Two plus two always equals four. A particular combination of notes creates a specific musical sound. Water consists of one oxygen and two hydrogen atoms.

However, other facts are only correct until we discover new facts, and it takes someone with a different perspective to question what is considered "normal" to reveal the truth. For example, before Copernicus, scientists thought the sun moved around the earth. After years of study, Copernicus went out on a limb and suggested that the earth revolved around the sun. His ideas were branded as heresy, yet his theory is now known as fact.

There are some facts that even science can't prove. No one denies gravity exists. We all know it works. However, science has yet to figure out exactly why.[3]

Things get sticky, as they always do, when it comes to people. We are motivated to act based on our understanding of what is right or wrong, which may not be straightforward. Indeed, both good and bad behavior may be tied to the same value. For instance, acts of both charity and revenge can be motivated by a sense of equality. In the act of charity, we attempt to help create equality through monetary gifts or donating our time. In the act of revenge, we attempt to create equality by getting even. "If I do this to that person, then we are even."

Almost every moment of every day, we are influenced by current events. The media plays a large part in this, but our families, neighbors, social groups, places of work and worship all come into the mix. We tend to accept the sources we trust as right and dismiss the sources we do not as wrong, cementing our confirmation bias. Every country, every region, every city has a bias in their media, and we are fed what someone else thinks is important. People deal in misinformation and lies to prove their point or purposely destroy others' reputations. If we are only willing to listen to information that confirms our own beliefs and understanding, we might unconsciously default to incorrect information—accepting information as factual that is not.

Balancing Commonalities and Differences

The nature of diversity is difference. As we consider diversity within our organizations, we look to who is and who is not represented. We want to figure out how to get the right blend of differences to satisfy the government, our customers, and our stockholders.

And yet, differences can be contentious. We need to decide which differences deserve our focus. When measuring differences, we must consider, "Different from whom?" And we all know the answer to that question: The majority population is the standard by which we are measuring.

This approach to diversity only causes divisiveness. In its most benign form, it creates the false notion, "If I look like the majority, then I am not diverse." It puts the majority population on the defensive rather than helping them become advocates for diversity. In its most malignant form, employees from the majority group see visibly diverse people in the organization and look at them as "filling in boxes." For those majority people, diversity now becomes something to fight against because they don't perceive it as including them.

Conversely, if I am not from the majority group, then I am "different," and when a diversity program highlights how I am different, I stand out more. Of course, no one wants to feel somebody hired them simply to check a box. This practice puts people on the defensive; they seek to justify their role, their skills, and any promotions they get. For them, diversity becomes exhausting—yet another systemic issue they must navigate.

Diversity in organizations need not only be about differences, but also how we balance the differences with the things we have in common. We create connections and build relationships through the things we have in common; we recognize that creativity and innovation are born from our different perspectives.

To build efficient and effective working relationships, we must push beyond our initial response to an individual's visible characteristics and understand that although someone may not look like us or may have a different background, we still have things in common. When we take time to talk to each other, we might discover we have much more in common than we initially thought.

Once we find commonalities, it can be very tempting to never talk about differences. I often hear, "Why do we have to focus on the differences? Doesn't that just cause problems?" Yes. Only focusing on differences *can* cause problems. At the same time, focusing only on the things we have in common leads to compliance, which comes in two forms. In the first, we expect others to yield to our ideas and ways of doing things. In the second, we accommodate others simply to get along within the system. Neither form is conducive to an engaging and productive work environment.

Consequently, diversity efforts are about achieving that just-right balance between commonalities and differences.

It's important to understand, "We all want to be respected," and still know there are differences in how we show respect.

It's important to believe, "We all want to be successful," and to remember we all define "success" differently.

It's important to recognize, "We are all human," yet still grasp the historical and systemic challenges faced by different groups.

When we have a more holistic understanding of diversity, our commonalities lead to connection, and our differences lead to new ways of seeing and experiencing the world. Relationships built on commonalities, and the unique perspectives discovered through differences, lead not only to the creativity and innovation we need in our organizations, but also to inclusion.

The next time you find yourself focusing only on a colleague's differences, stop and try to find some commonalities. And, when you notice yourself homing in on commonalities, ask about some differences.

We find true diversity, and inclusion, in the balance of the two.

Completing Step 3:
Make a Conscious Effort to Learn Different Perspectives

Human beings are naturally more comfortable around people who look and act like them. Widening our circle to include people who may be quite different from us takes a conscious effort, making many of us uncomfortable. Take advantage of all the online opportunities available to learn about different life experiences and points of view, or go to the online portal at www.TheDWordDiversity.com for more suggestions.

I often get asked, "How can I *possibly* know about everyone else's differences?" It's easy to get overwhelmed, but not all differences matter. It doesn't matter if you wore a blue shirt and your colleague wore a white shirt to work today. Instead, what might matter are things like race/ethnicity, gender, age, socio-economic status, ability, religion. These are *the differences that make a difference.*

As you work through the suggestions below, focus on *differences that can make a difference* as you interact with others, rather than trivial differences like shirt color.

- Seek to discover commonalities *and* differences. Talk to someone who seems quite different from you. Find at least three commonalities. Similarly, talk to someone who seems very much like you and find three significant differences.

- Stop making assumptions about people, especially those with whom you've had limited interaction. Don't assume you know everything they're going through. If you're not sure, ask. A simple "Can you help me understand?" will help you avoid a myriad of misunderstandings.

- Pick a value you listed in Step 1 and talk about it with another person. Is that value a priority for them? How do they express it in their day-to-day life? Is their expression the same, or different, from yours? How might the differences have caused a misunderstanding had you not had this conversation? Remember to share your perspective, too. Being vulnerable is vital to building authentic connections.

Having Conversations

Step 4:

*We accept we cannot resolve our differences
by pointing fingers and placing blame.
We are committed to learning how to have conversations
about our differences.*

Two people looking at the same thing never see the same thing.

Suppose we're sitting at a baseball park watching a game together. We both understand the basic rules of the game. Each team has nine active players. There is a diamond containing a pitcher's mound, home plate, and three bases. There is an infield and an outfield.

The pitcher throws the ball to the batter. The batter tries to hit the ball to reach a base, and advance other runners around the bases to score runs. The fielding team tries to stop the batting team by causing "outs." Each team gets three outs to try to score runs. Then the other team takes a turn. A sequence where each team has the opportunity to bat is called an "inning." One game has nine innings. At the end of the game, the team with the most runs wins.

Still, we see a different game. Maybe we're cheering for different teams. Maybe we have different favorite players. Maybe you see a strike, and I see a ball. (Of course, all that matters is what the umpire sees...)

We also bring different visceral meanings to the game. The smells and sounds at the ballpark are different from those we would experience if we watched the game at home or in a bar. Maybe you have memories of sneaking into games with your friends as a child. Maybe attending baseball games was a special event that I shared with my brother. Maybe you played baseball in college, and attending games remind you of your glory days. These different scenarios make "how" we see the game unique for each of us.

Now, imagine all the perspectives that each of us brings to a simple everyday life event. When we experience the event, we may agree about certain aspects at face level, but we may not agree at a deeper level and never even discuss the issue further.

This is where misunderstandings originate.

When we think we agree on events, or directions at work, or rules of conduct, or ethics, but we never discuss the deeper meaning, we open ourselves up to potential misunderstandings.

We Only Know What We Know

We all know people who think it's acceptable to yell at other people. They take pride in pointing their finger at someone who is doing something "wrong" and confronting the person with the error of their ways. I've been in discussion groups and classes where people have been humiliated for asking a question. They are scolded, "How could you *not* know?!" as if everyone has access to the same information and same life experiences.

Unity cannot be achieved without understanding each other's perspectives. We can make plenty of assumptions about what we *think* others have experienced, but we don't know until we have discussed it.

There are many books available describing how to have effective conversations, and, later in this chapter, I will give you an overview of my process based on compassion. However, there are a few basic concepts to understand first.

Diversity Tough Love:

There's no such thing as "normal."

"Normal" is different for each of us. None of us knows anything other than what we have directly learned or experienced. Period.

If you're raised in a community where everyone looks pretty much just like you, then that's what "normal" is to you. You're a fish in the water.

You need to take yourself out of the water to see things from a different perspective. When you create new experiences—such as watching a movie or reading a book that you wouldn't typically read; taking a vacation to a place you haven't been; or moving someplace new—you experience something novel and can see your community in a new light.

For example, I live in a small, mostly White town in the Midwestern United States. Many people in my town have grown up here and never left, and they have a lot of trouble understanding racism. Perhaps a person's only experience with Mexican people is what they see on television or experience at the all-inclusive resort where they vacationed. How can that person possibly have a complete understanding of the racism that exists towards Mexican people in the United States? Moreover, if they have a Mexican friend, the friend may not be comfortable sharing stories with them because they're unlikely to believe it. After all, they've never experienced it.

Yes, there are many available facts and figures that prove systemic racism exists, but the sad reality is that facts and figures rarely convince anyone of anything. It's how we *feel* about it that matters. You can scream and yell all you like, but unless a person has experienced racism first-hand or witnessed a friend being targeted by it, racism means nothing to them. (Remember those Degrees of Separation? We're not particularly good at caring about people beyond two degrees.[1])

To be clear, this is not an excuse or an apology—it's reality, and I rarely see people who are willing to step into this perspective to understand.

I was in a discussion group recently where we were talking about racism. A Latina member said (I have permission to use her story, but she wished to remain anonymous), "I grew up in an all Latin neighborhood, and I didn't think racism existed, either. It wasn't part of my reality because I never really left the neighborhood. Then, we took a family vacation to Branson, Missouri. My family is pretty light-skinned, and we blended in—until my grandma spoke Spanish to me in the store, and for the rest of the time we were in that store, we were treated differently from when we came into the store."

We often want to punish people for what they don't know, but that is not fair. Firing someone for saying something out of ignorance is not fair. Firing someone for saying something to be cruel and demeaning is fair. Knowing the difference requires discernment, which we'll cover more in Step 7.

What's this mean for business?[2]

When we assume someone is "just like me," we think they have the same wants, needs, and motivations we do. We decide who is (and

---

[2] The discussion about Compassionate Diversity® and the steps for having compassionate conversations are reprinted with permission from my chapter, "The Hidden Cost of Doing Business," published in: Mongan, M. (Ed.). (2020). *Brilliant Breakthroughs for the Small Business Owner: Fresh Perspectives on Profitability, People, Productivity, and Finding Peace in Your Business.*[2]

isn't) qualified for a job based on whether or not they act as we do. We coach them by telling them what worked for us. We measure their performance by *our* preferences for how things get done. We assume the products and services successful in one market should work in a new market. In the end, we miss out on good employees, squash innovation, and lose sales.

This is where Compassionate Diversity® comes in. Compassionate Diversity® is a comprehensive approach to seeing different perspectives, understanding others, and building bridges in understanding which incorporates both the head and the heart. We develop compassion and affect change through understanding what others truly need *from their perspective—not what we think they need.*

Fundamental to Compassionate Diversity® is the Compassionate Diversity® Solution Process:

- At the **Comprehension** level, we work to understand the reactions and expectations of ourselves and others, and the purpose and outcomes of the situation.
- At the **Connection** level, we work to create shared meaning and alignment of purpose.
- In **Collaboration**, we develop more innovative and sustainable solutions in our businesses and in our communities by creating more compassionate environments.

Putting the Compassionate Diversity® Solution Process Into Action

The Compassionate Diversity® Solution Process moves compassion into action. Whenever we're in a new situation or place of conflict, we can use this process to move forward effectively.

First, the ground rules:

- **All perspectives are valid, even if you disagree with them.** We all come to our viewpoints through complex processes informed by our learning and life experiences. No path, therefore, no perspective, is less valid than any other.

- **Your focus is to understand, inform, and resolve.** You are not trying to convince anyone of anything because right/wrong arguments lead to polarization.

- **It's okay not to know.** We live in a world where saying, "I don't know," or, "Let me get back to you," means we're stupid, or we don't know what we're doing. Inclusion work requires vulnerability. Vulnerability allows us the space necessary to say, "I don't know." This can be difficult to do, especially for business leaders, but *admitting our vulnerability helps build trust.*[3] (Step 8 covers vulnerability in more detail.)

Comprehension

The first step in Comprehension is emotional awareness. Our emotions are our internal guidance system. They tell us whether we are in or out of alignment with our beliefs, values, and expectations (BVE). If we're feeling good in a particular situation, then it means we are in alignment with our BVE. If we're not feeling good, then we're out of alignment. It's that simple. *(We'll discuss the importance of Emotional Intelligence in Step 10.)*

Next, take inventory of your BVE. What are your beliefs about the situation? What are your expectations? What might others involved be thinking and feeling?

Now, we need to understand the deeper purpose and desired outcomes of the situation. For instance, if we're interviewing a candidate, the purpose isn't to ask questions and gather answers. Our purpose is to find the best person for the job. How might our biases get in the way of accomplishing this purpose?

Connection

We want to use the information we gathered in Comprehension to create shared meaning and alignment to purpose. It's essential we connect before there's a more significant gap in understanding, and you miss out on the next sale, lose another employee, or allow conflict to get out of hand. CAUTION: *We are not trying to solve anything at this stage.* Resist the temptation to jump in with any conclusions. We may even need to occasionally revisit Comprehension as we go through this Connection step.

First, decide what is out of alignment. Are your BVE out of alignment with the purpose of the situation? Are your BVE out of alignment with others? We often try to change people to conform to our perspective when it's the process, or maybe even us, that needs to change. If it's you who needs straightening out, then get into alignment with the purpose of the situation and move on to Collaboration.

If alignment is necessary with others, then it is time to begin conversations. Remember the ground rules of this process, and first identify the things you have in common. You may find the gap is not as wide as you perceived. Once you have found common ground, begin talking about the differences.

Don't default into defending your position. Instead, ask questions like:

- "Can you tell me more?"
- "What else would you like me to know about this?"
- "What more do you want to know from me?"

CRITICAL: *Listen to understand and resist every urge you have to refute what you're hearing.* Doing so only ends up polarizing the discussion, deteriorating trust, and increasing frustration. We cannot convince each other through facts alone when we're in the heat of conflict. When you're feeling frustrated and want to jump in, focus on your heart and slow down your breathing.

Shifting focus to our hearts gets us out of our heads and helps us think more clearly by bringing our heart rhythm into a more coherent state. We can listen without judgment and really hear what the other side is saying.

Finally, don't expect the other person to be the only one to change. Be open to modifying your expectations along the way.

Collaboration

When we understand the situation and feel we have all the information we need to make an appropriate decision, we can move on to *Collaboration*. Here, we take appropriate action to drive desired outcomes. There are only two outcomes: 1) change; or 2) no change. "Change" means we need to create a new process or system. "No change" means we maintain the status quo, but with a new understanding. This may mean accepting some things we may disagree with or letting go of other long-held beliefs. (Step 11 can help you with letting go.)

Give yourself—and others—a break!

We can read about theories and concepts—but theory and reality are two completely different things. We aren't good at talking about our differences because we haven't practiced having conversations about those differences. It's human nature to be uncomfortable talking about topics we know little about. We don't want to offend others. We worry that we may look stupid or get embarrassed. However, until we can practice, we can't embody theoretical lessons. Like it or not, learning about how to have conversations about our differences works the same way. People will mess up—*you* will mess up. This doesn't mean we excuse bad behavior; however, we must learn to discern between appropriate actions regarding punishment and learning opportunities.

Diversity Tough Love:

If you want to remain comfortable, you will never learn.

We learn best by making mistakes. When we get to Step 11, we'll talk about forgiveness and letting go. For now, if someone else messes up, please don't throw it in their face; and if you mess up, take a deep breath, own it, apologize, and figure out what you learned.

The Things We Can Learn From Each Other

Compassion arises when we are motivated to relieve the suffering of another. Before taking action, we must be grounded in understanding the perspectives and experiences of those we wish to help. If we are not, the action we take is motivated by our desire to relieve our discomfort with the situation, and our efforts will likely fall flat. We must understand the system within which the suffering was created from all perspectives. Having discussions and sharing our stories are integral parts of this understanding.

I've been doing D&I work for over 20 years, and I see my BIPOC family and friends are exhausted. They're tired of the burden they've had to carry for generations. Tired of being the token representative. Tired of suppressing who they are in order to fit in—and tired of being suppressed.

Many White people have approached me because they don't know what to do or say. They're told, "Educate yourself!" and they're trying to do so. They see their Black friends hurting, and they don't want to add to their pain. They're standing up in the best way they know how to their racist friends and family members, and yet, they often struggle with what to say. To those folks, I say, "Don't stop! Don't ever stop! This is hard work, but stopping is a privilege that isn't afforded to your Black friends."

Our world would be a much better place if we would all listen to and believe each other's stories and experiences. There's so much for us to learn from each other and so much that we can share. While you may think you know everything about a person's experience based on the way they look, you are only assuming you know unless you talk to them.

We must hear the stories of the underserved and underprivileged. Stories of the majority population are at the forefront because of our society's systemic issues. We hear an overabundance of those stories, and they become "normal." The only way we expand "normal" is by listening to and believing everyone's stories and elevating the voices of those who historically have been silenced.

Regardless of where you are in the system, accept that when someone tells you their experience, it is true for them, even if it isn't true for you. Denying another person's experience discredits them and does more to harm than to heal.

Completing Step 4:
Having Conversations

We're taught to be colorblind and gender blind and not to acknowledge other's abilities or backgrounds, *but our discomfort with discussing these issues is proof itself that these issues are important.* We must participate in conversations if we want to learn. If we don't practice talking about complex topics, we'll never get good at it.

There's just one suggestion for this chapter:

Engage in conversations. If you implement the ground rules alone, you will make great strides. Practice the three steps of the Compassionate Diversity® Solution Process—Comprehension, Connection, and Collboration. When you feel a need to explain, ask more questions instead. When you make a mistake, own it, apologize, and move on. Don't forget to grant others grace, as well.

(You can find more stories and references in the online portal, www.TheDWordDiversity. com—as well as a brief session on resilience.)

A Win-Win Proposition

Step 5:

We discover when we can achieve fair outcomes, everyone benefits.
We release notions of equality and act with equity.

If you live in the United States, you're probably aware of the free and reduced lunch program for economically disadvantaged children. Are you aware there's a School Breakfast Program[1], also?

In 1966, the United States Department of Agriculture began a two-year pilot program sponsored by Kentucky representative Carl Perkins. Perkins wanted to help rural children "who got up early to work the fields with their parents and arrived at school hungry after long bus rides."[2]

Few people know that at the same time, the Black Panther Party was organizing a Free Breakfast for Children Program out of a church in Oakland, California, as a response to the government's declared war on poverty. They felt the initiatives to end poverty did not extend to the Black community, so they took matters into their own hands and began serving breakfast for children out of the basement of a local church in 1968.[3]

The School Breakfast Program pilot was extended a few times, and it became permanent in 1975.[4]

What started as separate programs to benefit specific groups of children was expanded to serve free and reduced breakfasts for all economically disadvantaged children.

Diversity is Not a Zero-Sum Game

Too often, diversity is viewed as a win/lose proposition. If one group "gets" something, then another group "loses" something.

From the majority perspective, introducing a diversity strategy and implementing goals means they will have to give something up. They see no benefit in diversity because they think diversity isn't about them. There is no WIIFM ("What's in it for me?") and no connection to the need for diversity goals.

Diversity strategies create problems on the non-majority side, as well. Instead of "gaining something," thanks to majority resentment, they are even more convinced they were hired to satisfy demographic needs, not because of their skills. They may feel they constantly have to prove themselves in their jobs, which diverts their energy from day-to-day tasks.

It's a stressful situation for everyone. At its roots are power dynamics and limited mindsets. Consider this:

	Majority	Non-majority
Power Dynamic	When the system has been set up to benefit one group, leveling the playing field to make it equal for everyone sounds threatening and leads to denial. *"Everyone has equal opportunity. There's no such thing as systemic bias."*	When there are limited examples of "people like me" in leadership, then the majority approach "must be" the path to success. *"In order to 'fit' into the system, I must conform as much as possible to majority expectations. I must act like they do, even though I don't look or think as they do."*
Limited Mindset	When equity is seen as a threat, it leads to fear. *"I must make every effort to hold onto 'my' job because someone else might take it."* (This might even include believing, perhaps unconsciously, that, *"Only certain people are capable of doing jobs like mine,"* or, *"I work best with people who are just like me."*)	When one finds glass ceilings everywhere, it's easy to get discouraged. *"There is only so far I can go in any particular job. I'll never get ahead."*

These beliefs may be deeply rooted and hard to overcome, but diversity is not a zero-sum game.

Diversity Tough Love:

Diversity is not a zero-sum game.

Diversity is a win/win proposition.

Once we get clear on Steps 2 and 3—that diversity is about non-majority and majority; others and myself; differences and commonalities—then we begin to see the intersectionality of diversity. (Intersectionality is the interconnectedness of all diversity elements, for example, race, class, and gender, that combine to make us who we are.) When we contemplate the complex web of our identity and what each of us brings in terms of advantages and disadvantages, we can begin to understand that diversity leads to greater benefits for everyone.

Study after study has shown this to be true about diversity. Just a few examples:

— In the United States, much legislation around equal employment and nondiscrimination came out of the civil rights movement. The Pregnancy Discrimination Act was signed into law in 1978, and companies implemented maternity leave and other employee benefits to aid working mothers. In turn, those laws and benefits have grown into paternity and family leave, which benefit everyone.[5]

— Globally, studies show that the more women there are in the workforce, the higher the country's gross domestic product (GDP). In the United States, achieving gender parity has the potential to add $4.3 trillion to the economy by 2025.[6]

— Diversity drives innovation. Diverse companies are 45 percent more likely to report year-over-year growth and 70 percent more likely to have captured a new market. Expanding companies keep people employed and hire more people to support their growth.[7]

Some benefits of diversity in the workforce may be evident and immediate, and some may take more time. Just because one group is helped doesn't mean another is hurt. Instead, we find the changes made with diversity in mind are synergistic—when we give support to aid one group, we all eventually prosper.

Addressing Systemic Issues

We're all part of the same system. We all play into the game, regardless of which side we're on or if we understand the game or not. We are all subject to a system of inequity and exclusion. The question is, when will we all wake up and no longer play into it?

The COVID-19 pandemic has been devastating to people around the world. Here in the United States, Black, Indigenous, and People of Color (BIPOC) have been disproportionately affected by the disease. A study conducted by Harvard University researchers found that if the United States had paid reparations to descendants of Black slaves "well before the pandemic and lessened the equity gap between Black [sic] and Whites, coronavirus transmission in Louisiana could've been reduced between 31% and 68% for residents of all races."[8] (The state of Louisiana is historically a slave state and remains highly segregated based on race.)

Diversity Tough Love:

Systemic issues are real, and they affect everyone.

Denying systemic issues exist is much like being a climate denier today. There is tangible proof of issues that have existed for years. Organizations don't have equal leadership representation across gender, race/ethnicity, or any other standard we want to measure; laws are written which exclude rights and ensure inequities for portions of the population; and on and on.

The issues of our system cause stress. When we judge each other and argue with each other, we are under stress. When non-majority folks are passed over for a job or other economic opportunities because of who they are, it causes stress. When majority folks don't value equity and equality and exclaim, "They're taking our jobs!" they are under stress.

No organism can live in stress and survival mode indefinitely without consequences to its health. And when individuals are unhealthy, the system itself becomes unhealthy.

We've had a very unhealthy system for a very long time.

Real change requires finding a new way to do things—not just shoring up and fixing old systems. We can master Step 4 and have great conversations about building bridges across differences, but if those bridges are cracked at the foundation, they'll never hold the new structure. The only solution is to tear it down and build anew.

How do we do that? Here are the basic skills needed to create change that would benefit everyone:

1. Pay attention to where you focus. Our brains don't know the difference between an event we are experiencing or one we keep playing over and over in our heads. Whether it's happening "live" or it's imagined, we have the same physical reactions and release the same stress hormones. We must keep our focus on what we want to create. *(There's more detail on this at the end of this chapter.)*

2. Build resilience. Bad things happen to everybody, and we're often caught off guard when they do. It's essential to have a store of personal energy to see us through difficult times and help us recover from them. Resilience offers us the opportunity to get back on track. *(We'll cover the importance of building resilience in Step 8.)*

3. Learn discernment. Discernment is the key to understanding every issue. Just a few things to start discerning:

- When we're in survival mode, and when we're not, so we can determine the most effective way to focus our energy.

- When we're in an environment committed to cooperation and growth, and when we're not, so we have the support we need to express our talents and live to our full potential.

- When old habits and ways of thinking are more harmful to us than living with the discomfort needed to bring about change.

4. Practice compassion. Compassion isn't an excuse to ignore all the bad stuff going on. It can be more work than our old worn-out way of trying to get things done because it requires us to take time to understand other people *from their perspective,* not our own.

Equality versus Equity

We ignore diversity when we strive to treat everyone "the same." It turns out, "the same" and "with equity" are two different things. It's difficult to treat everyone with equity because we must understand other perspectives and discern different contexts. Understanding takes time and effort, so it becomes much easier to implement zero-tolerance policies. The same punishment applies for the same infraction, regardless of the circumstances. Simple. No thinking involved—everyone is treated the same.

We likely do more harm than good when we minimize situations to one solution. Zero-tolerance policies are not even-handed when they mete out the same consequences for uneducated or inexperienced people versus people who are truly being cruel or obnoxious. When we fail to see the diversity of reasons why people might violate a rule, we end up creating solutions that don't work. As a result, our challenges perpetuate themselves and never truly get resolved.

Equal and equitable treatments are not the same. We think we're fair when we treat people the same, but not everyone wants to be treated the same, nor does every situation call for the same treatment. If you've got children, you know that one might be more artistically gifted, while another excels at math. The artistic one might need a tutor to get through math class. Equal treatment would mean we need to get a math tutor for the other child, too, even though she doesn't need it. Equitable treatment means getting the math genius the help she needs in history class because that's where she needs it, or maybe even no help at all if all her grades are fine.

We encourage the strengths of our children. We don't expect them to be the same, and we recognize when they need help and get them the help they need. Why do we expect all our employees to be the same, and treat them the same way, and call that fair?

One Small Shift that Makes All The Difference

Society is very polarized, and it's easy to feel our security is threatened. Some of the threats are real, and some of them are imagined. At every turn, we think that we need to protect ourselves—from other people, from politicians, from our environment, and from whatever else is distressing us.

Where we focus our attention matters.

We spend so much time *fighting against* things that we can be left feeling overloaded and exhausted. But when we feel threatened to our very core, what alternative do we have?

How about trying *standing for?*

It's a subtle but powerful shift. For example:

- Do you fight against hate—or stand for love?
- Do you fight against discrimination—or stand for equity?
- Do you fight against immigration bans—or stand for human dignity?

The positive feelings of "standing for" are more beneficial for us—in terms of our mental, emotional, physical, and spiritual health—than the negative emotions generated by "fighting against."

Understanding and focusing on the difference between "fighting against" and "standing for" takes a healthy dose of self-awareness and self-regulation. It's not easy.

To figure out where you stand, ask yourself:

- Do you find things wrong to criticize, or do you find things right to support?
- Are you more full of negative feelings, like hate and anger, or more full of empathy and compassion? (On the spectrum of emotions, even "sadness" is softer than hate, so if you can't make it to empathy, take one step at a time.)
- Do you spend more time telling people how things *should be* or listening to people about how things *are* for them?

These are very personal questions. Answering them requires us to be vulnerable and honest with ourselves about our beliefs and values. And that might shake the core of who we are.

But times like these are all about change—change for individuals and the world. If you want to leave the world a better place by working in more compassionate ways, then letting go of old ways is the only way to do it. We've spent our human history fighting against. Maybe it's time we start standing for.

Completing Step 5: Moving to Win/Win

Recent research shows humans are not only cooperative but also compassionate by nature.[9] Feeling compassion for others causes our heart rate to go down and oxytocin levels to rise. Helping others gives us as much satisfaction as helping ourselves.

What has this got to do with power dynamics and limited mindsets?

When we focus on win/win solutions, both become moot. I begin to see that each person in the group, myself included, is valuable for who they are and the experiences they bring. I see potential limitations in how far I can get on my own, but the more successful my group, the further I can go. As a result, we work to ensure everyone in the group has what they need to be productive.

Below are a few ideas to help promote a win/win mindset. For exercises on shifting from equality to equity, be sure to visit the online portal at www.TheDWordDiversity.com.

- Examine your beliefs around diversity. Where do you fall in the Power Dynamic/Limited Mindset chart? How can you challenge your beliefs around power dynamics and limited mindsets? How can you challenge the views of others?

- Mentor/be mentored by someone different from you in some significant way. Mentoring doesn't need to be a top-down power process. Whatever your position within the company, you can mentor and be mentored by others to understand different perspectives.

- Take an honest look at your organization's policies and practices. What needs to change to create a more inclusive organization? Do job descriptions and recruiting policies need updating? Do you have a problem retaining certain groups of employees? What policies have sat unquestioned for years, simply because, "It's the way we've always done it?"

Becoming Aware

Step 6:

We work to build a better understanding of ourselves because knowing who we are is key to understanding each other.

You might think we addressed the hard stuff in the first five steps, as we touched on bias, privilege, and systemic inequities. The next seven steps outline skills you need to build to be more culturally competent.

What is cultural competence? Cultural competence is the ongoing process of discovering cultural patterns of beliefs and behaviors in oneself and others and using those patterns to develop more innovative and sustainable solutions. When we are culturally competent, we can balance the similarities and differences between ourselves and others to communicate, resolve conflict, and solve problems more effectively.

One of the things I hear most often from majority culture people is, "I don't have a culture." They think this because their culture *is* the culture—it's "normal." However, normal is relative to our individual experiences, as we've discussed.

I invite you to think very broadly of culture as the beliefs, values, and behaviors we learn from the groups of people we belong to. The groups influencing us may be based on race/ethnicity, gender, sexual orientation, or generation. They may also be the places we've lived, what we studied in school, or even our parental status. We learn group norms and unwritten rules of engagement within these groups.

It's easy to think, "Everyone else is just like me," and we don't typically realize they aren't until we disagree. We may be able to avoid this trap if we have a good sense of "what influenced me." In this step, we're going to build our awareness.

Getting Aware About Awareness

Awareness is the necessary first step to solve any challenges we're having. Unfortunately, we're usually only snapped into awareness when something happens to interrupt our routine.

Awareness is a broad concept. For The 12 Steps to Diversity Recovery™, we're not talking about being aware of the 12 Steps—as in "Heart Disease Awareness Month." We're talking about a more personal kind of awareness, including self-awareness, mindfulness, and other-awareness.

- **Self-awareness:** Too often with diversity, we want to jump straight to understanding "them," and we forget that we see every interaction we have through our own lens. Our lens includes the values, beliefs, and behaviors we have learned through the years. As we explored in Step 1, our lens shapes how we decide what is "right" and "wrong." Self-awareness is about discovering your own diversity.

- **Mindfulness:** Mindfulness is awareness of our current situation and reactions. It's a form of self-awareness that's practiced in the present moment. Being mindful in situations helps us connect our heads and hearts and regulate our emotions, responses, and actions better. Mindfulness techniques in diversity & inclusion classes "can help us become more aware of our biases and reduce them," as well as help us better regulate emotions in challenging situations.[1]

- **Other-awareness:** We make assumptions about what other people are thinking or what motivates their actions based on our own knowledge and experience. However, we don't know if our assumptions are right or wrong unless we ask. Building our "other-awareness" helps us to understand their perspectives. When we understand different perspectives, we understand there's no such thing as a "one size fits all" solution. Other-awareness forces us to think about the best solution within the context of the given situation. *(We'll look at "context" more in the next step.)*

The goal of awareness is to bring attention to our assumptions and the needs of others so we can see different perspectives and, perhaps, change our approach. While we want to be mindful of many things as we work through these twelve steps, the most foundational piece is self-awareness. We will focus on that for the remainder of this chapter.

Why Self-Awareness?

Every self-help book, every method for personal change, every 12-step program requires self-awareness. No matter what we want to improve upon, self-awareness is always a required component. How do we see the world? What do we value, and where did we learn it? How do we behave around those values? We need to understand our own story to understand better our own perspective of the world.

Too often, when working with people, we want to jump straight to understanding "them," and we forget we see every interaction we have through our own lens. That lens includes the values, beliefs, and behaviors we have been taught by the many groups to which we belong (our "cultures"). Our lens shapes how we decide what is "right" and what is "wrong." In Step 2, we discovered we are all diverse. Self-awareness is about discovering *your* diversity.

> ## Diversity Tough Love:
>
> *Diversity isn't all about "them."*
> *We must continually practice self-awareness if we want to be more*
> *culturally competent.*

Learning more about ourselves can be risky. Why? Whenever we build our self-awareness, we might find out some things about ourselves that we don't like. That's hard to take, but it's also an essential part of understanding what we might want to change. Without looking inside to understand our own perspectives, we can't discover the hidden biases that might be holding us back from being more effective in our work.

Who, Me, Change?

One of the most common questions I get in seminars and from people I coach is, "Who has to change?" or a similar, more defensive version, "Why do *I* have to change?"

My short answer? "You can't force anyone else to change because you only control yourself. It's up to you."

I'm sure we've all thought, "Why can't they change to accommodate me?" We want other people to change to our liking, and sometimes we even try to force them to do our will. We think we can control things outside of us, but we all know that's not possible. We may *influence* others, but the only person we completely control is ourselves.

Humans are conscious beings. Not only can we think and act, but we can also observe our thoughts and actions. That means we're responsible for what we do and what we don't do. It also means we're capable of conscious change.

However, we have to want to change—no one can do that for us. We also must have a reason for the change. Usually, we choose to change when old ways of thinking or acting are more harmful than living with the discomfort of change. If what we are doing works for us, we find no need to change.

For example, there are people in my town who have lived here their entire lives and do not believe they are racist. They rant about "those people," then close with, "I'm not racist. I have never caused harm to a Black person." Given their life experience, they have never encountered many BIPOC people. They do not think they need to change because their beliefs are not challenged and have not caused them any discomfort.

My town has grown quite a bit in the years I've lived here. More people are moving in from other areas. Children who grew up here and went away to college have returned. These groups bring a wider range of perspectives and are beginning to challenge the status quo. They're making it uncomfortable for racist views to be expressed. People living here with those views have two choices: 1) live with their discomfort when challenged and continue to defend their views, or 2) be open to listening and learning more about how to adjust their views.

When something isn't working and we bump up against a challenge, we must stop and think. Solving problems requires being in the moment. You can't be thinking about what you're going to cook for dinner, where you're going to go this weekend, or anything else. You must be present to solve a problem.

We can't change anything unless we are aware there is a problem, and we must recognize *our* role in that problem to effect change.

To be clear: *You have a role in any challenge you bump up against.* It's not all about the other person and "their problem." You are experiencing a challenge because you have something to learn. Think about it—if you knew what to do, you wouldn't be having a problem, would you? The solution to your challenge starts with **you**. It is your responsibility to take control of what is in your control—yourself, your reactions, your experiences, your learning.

Diversity Tough Love:

Stop worrying about everyone else.
You are the only one who needs to change.

If you are not aware of what *you* are contributing to the challenge, you cannot know what you need to do to help solve it. If you don't understand why you think what you think and why you react the way you do, how can you understand anyone else?

Understanding others starts with understanding ourselves.

Mirror, Mirror on the Wall

We often use the term "mirroring" to describe reflecting someone else's actions or feelings back to them—we mirror their posture or facial expressions to get a better sense of what they are feeling. We can also use mirroring as a tool for developing our self-awareness.

Mirroring helps us develop empathy for another person because of the mirror neurons in our brain, which fire when we observe someone else doing something. (We briefly discussed mirror neurons in Step 1.) For example, when we see someone pick up a pencil, the neurons that fire are some of the same neurons that fire when *we* physically pick up a pencil. These neurons help us to not only understand the actions of other people but also to discern their possible intentions. Think of it as catching someone else's mood. If someone smiles at you, you get a "feeling" of "smile," and (hopefully!) you smile back.

We can also look at "mirroring" from another angle. Not only can we reflect others' feelings back to them, but we can use others to reflect our qualities back to us. We know that our perspective comes from the things we have learned and experienced. It makes sense then that we can't see qualities in others that we, ourselves, do not have.

That may sound like good news to some. To others, it may not. Even things that annoy us most about others are *qualities we have.*

Mirroring reflects our direct experience right back to us. When we see someone as joyful, we reflect the joy within ourselves. When we see someone as angry, we reflect the anger within ourselves. When we notice qualities in other people, we can ask ourselves, "What piece of that quality do I have?" because, rest assured, you have it somewhere in you.

Mirroring is a powerful tool for self-awareness and self-reflection. It is also key to our misinterpretation of others. When we disagree with someone, we tend to think it's a faulty way in which they are approaching the subject. With mirroring, we discover the issue may be with us and how we are experiencing the world. When we read an article or email or post that sounds angry, we may wonder why the author is so angry. Maybe it's just our own anger reflected back to us. The concept of mirroring would require us to ask, "Why am I so angry?"

With mirroring, we can discern whether we are open to valuing and respecting other perspectives. If we are angry, mirroring helps us recognize we are closed-minded. When we are at peace, we know we are better positioned to appreciate differences and make better decisions.

Intent and Impact

Diversity Tough Love:

Your intentions rarely matter.
What's more important is how your actions impact others.

We're all human, and sometimes we say or do foolish things. No one is immune. We often say we don't "intend" to hurt someone or do something thoughtless, but whether we intend it or not, the impact of what we say or do is felt by other people. Building our self-awareness can help us align our intended messages to impact others positively rather than negatively.

If we keep hurting other people with our words or actions, at some point, we have to stop hiding behind "I didn't intend to do that." When we keep bumping up against reactions and challenges we did not intend to cause, we must understand our actions are negatively impacting others.

"That's not what I intended" may be an excuse the first time, but not the tenth. Once you know the impact of your words or actions, adjusting them is up to you. When we continue to do something "unintentionally," even after we are aware of the effect of our actions, doesn't it then become "intentional"? If we don't change how we're acting or what we're doing or saying, we're intentionally choosing to remain ignorant of ourselves, our motivations, and the effect of our words and actions on others.

If we are not self-aware and keep running into the same problems, we're just deliberately unaware. It's within your control to become conscious of what you're doing and change your behavior to ensure the intent of your words and actions aligns with the impact on others.

Every Moment is a Choice

We all have them—friends who love to post on social media about how miserable they are. They hate their jobs; they don't like where they live; they're frustrated with their family.

I believe everything is a choice, and there are two types of choices: conscious and unconscious. Unconscious choices can also be called habits. They're the things we've done so often they're just second nature, like driving the same route to work every day. They're also the ones feeding into unconscious biases and our actions towards each other. Conscious choices are the ones we stop to think about, and they typically come up because our unconscious choices get interrupted. Making decisions to drive home from work a different way because you've got to stop at the grocery store is a conscious choice. All day long, we shift between unconscious and conscious choices.

We are an accumulation of the choices we have made. I am writing this book because I chose to do diversity and inclusion work over twenty years ago. I made choices along the way to continue doing the work through good times and bad. Eventually, I chose to write a book and sign a contract with a publisher. Every day I sat down to write was a choice.

We tend to blame people or circumstances for things in our lives when the truth is those things are there because of the choices we have made. I do not wish to minimize the fact that some choices are tough, and there are times when we must choose the lesser of two evils. Leaving a job or a bad family situation may feel impossible, as doing so may result in undue hardship. We may not be able to change the situation immediately, but we can change how we respond within it and make smaller choices that may eventually lead to a more significant change.

It all comes down to self-awareness and control.

Closing out Step 6: Do We Choose Our Beliefs?

A friend once posed an interesting philosophical question: "Is a belief a choice?"

Beliefs are deeply held and ingrained in us at a very early age. We often act on them without even realizing that we do. We might be able to articulate *what* beliefs we hold, but we often can't explain *why* we believe what we believe.

Try this exercise. Very quickly, pick your top five beliefs. Below is a list of hot topics and values to get you started; if these don't fit, add your own.

- All people are/are not created equal
- Equality
- Integrity
- Global warming is/is not real
- Family
- Treating others the way I want to be treated
- Sexual orientation is/is not a choice
- Respect
- Capitalism/Socialism/Communism is superior to all other economic systems
- Excellence
- Innovation
- Helping others
- God and the Devil
- Loyalty
- People do/do not have a right to carry guns

Now, go back through the list, and take some time to journal about *why* you believe what you believe. Where did your beliefs originate? Have your beliefs evolved over time? Would you be willing to change your beliefs in light of new evidence?

This is where choice comes in. Faced with two possibilities—either I cling to my belief or change it in light of this new information—which do you choose?

(For more exercises on how to build your awareness, head out to the online portal: at www.TheDWordDiversity.com.)

Are You Who You Say You Are?

Step 7:

We discover we can remain true to ourselves while allowing others the space to be true to themselves.

I was sitting through my first performance review with my new boss. Under "Needs Improvement," the first item said, "Susan is too emotional."

I cried.

My boss became uncomfortable. He asked if I needed a break. I didn't. We forged ahead.

Over the years, the feedback of "Susan is too emotional" became a bit of a game for me. It was always there under the "Needs Improvement" section, but my boss found different ways to say it that weren't so direct. By my last year with him, it had morphed into, "I'm concerned for Susan's health."

I transferred into my new job. My new boss was again a man, but he was much more comfortable expressing emotions. We often had heated discussions about the projects we were working on and topics related to our work.

On my first performance review, the number one item under "Strengths" was my passion for my work.

What authenticity is—and is not

Cultural competence is not just about how we view other people and their behavior. It's also about building an awareness of how other people may see us. Are we true to our word? Do our actions reflect our values? It's important to recognize the last question is not, "Do our actions reflect what we *say*?" because what we *say* and what we *do* may be subject to cultural interpretation.

For example, let's look at the value of "hard work." We each have our own definition of hard work based on what we've individually experienced, observed, and learned. Suppose your boss assigns you to a new project, and you're excited to take it on. Which behavior do you consider "hard work"?

- Independently develop your plan for the project and execute it, depending on your boss as a sounding board and asking questions only when necessary; or
- Take the plan your boss has created and implement it, expecting to work closely with your boss to carry out their directives.

The answer? It depends.

The difference between the two answers given is the difference between behavior in egalitarian and hierarchical cultures.[1] In more egalitarian cultures, bosses rely on their employees. They trust their employees' experience and knowledge to get the job done, and they expect to be consulted only if the employee has challenges with the project.

Employees are expected to do as they are told in more hierarchical cultures. Micromanaging, which is frowned on in egalitarian cultures, is the norm. Bosses tend to be autocratic, and the boss/employee relationship is parental, with employees having an emotional tie to their superiors.

Authenticity is often misunderstood to mean many different things, like:

- Acting the same way in all situations.
- Being transparent.
- Always telling the truth.

However, these behaviors don't always reflect authentic behavior.

Diversity Tough Love:

Authenticity does not mean we act the same way in every situation.

Authenticity does not require us to act the same way in all situations. We may act differently at home than we do at work or when we're out with our friends. Does that make us inauthentic? Not necessarily. It means that we recognize our values can be expressed differently in different places.

In the previous example, we looked at the value of hard work. The bosses in both cultures value hard work. The difference is the *behavior* the bosses expect around hard work. When we only see through our cultural lens, we think there is only one way to express our values, and if we behave differently, we're inauthentic. However, suppose we were to shift our attention about what is authentic to the *value* instead of the *behavior*. We then recognize that we can remain authentic to our values, but we may need to readjust our behavior based on the context of the situation.

Authenticity does not mean transparency. Authenticity is often confused with transparency, but the two concepts are not related. Transparency is about openness, honesty, and accountability in business. We are transparent with information so people have everything they need to get their jobs done or make an informed decision.

Being authentic does not mean we must reveal all of our innermost thoughts and feelings. Spilling your guts may feel good, but it's not authentic.

In business, "Excessive sharing of information creates problems of information overload and can legitimize endless debate and second-guessing of senior executive decisions."[2] While certain information is helpful, unnecessary information is not. As a rule of thumb, it's best to share the information important *to* everyone *with* everyone; information specific to a specific department or role should be shared only there.

Authenticity is not necessarily the same as "telling the truth." Indeed, authenticity is about telling the truth *to yourself*, but it's not always necessary to tell the truth to others. (Did I hit a nerve with that statement? Good.)

Authenticity does not mean it's OK to hurt others. If what we have to say might be hurtful, then it's probably best left unsaid.

Discussions about telling the truth bump into the area of "political correctness." You can read more about this topic in the sidebar.

Diversity Tough Love:

"Choosing your words" carefully is not "political correctness."
It's valuing common humanity and showing respect.
Learn the difference.

We're All Tired of Political Correctness!

It's a hard truth to face, but people are not fundamentally good at understanding other people. We're not taught to understand ourselves and how our personal views were formed, much less how to understand people who are different from us. We develop our understanding of others through our learning and experience. It takes time, and trial and error. At best, those errors lead to embarrassment. At worst, it leads to losing one's job. Neither one is an optimal choice.

Until we work through the first six steps in this book, it's easy to assume everyone else is basically "just like me." We think, "Of course, everyone understands what 'respect' and 'integrity' mean. How can they not?" We say, "I treat other people like I want to be treated. After all, we're all just human." It's far less complicated to see how another person behaves and say, "That's wrong," than to think maybe it's just different and to explore some of those differences.

Political correctness (PC) challenges us to move beyond thinking "we're all the same" and consider another person's perspective. It flies in the face of "treating others like I want to be treated," which has a base assumption that we're all the same when we're not. It teaches that to get along, we have to tolerate each other and suppress speaking our truth, which is not easy to do if we fundamentally disagree with someone.

We think that political correctness is all about choosing our words carefully, for fear of saying the wrong thing and insulting someone. People say, "I'm tired of having to watch what I say! If I offend someone, then that's their problem."

Certainly, we can say anything we want to say, but we are not free from the consequences of what we say. If we say we value respect, then we must choose our words carefully so we do not unintentionally disrespect someone. If we're not willing to do that, then we need to re-evaluate whether "respect" is truly one of our values.

It's time to recognize our differences and no longer just say we value them, but show we do with our words and actions. When we can, we're on the road to being more inclusive.

So, what is authenticity?

Authenticity is the action we take based on our highest values.

Being authentic requires we:

- Are self-aware and clear about our values.
- Understand that values and behaviors are different things.
- Know that many behaviors express the same value.
- Recognize that different behaviors may be needed in different situations.
- Choose to act accordingly.

Authenticity means we narrow the gap between the person we show to the world and the person we truly are through living our values.

Using Discernment to Build Authenticity

A friend who is a college professor in the United States asked me, "I have Chinese foreign exchange students in my classes. When I read their assignments, the papers have similar thoughts, and sometimes, some of the passages are exactly the same. Why are they cheating?"

It all depends on your cultural perspective. People born and raised in the United States tend towards individualism. They value autonomous work, open discussions, and original ideas in school. In China, a more collectivist perspective is valued. Students are taught harmony, and individuals speak up to express the group's opinion.[3]

Questions like this intersect with ideas around morals and ethics. When we are culturally competent, we understand we don't have to agree with everyone to accept that their perspective is different from our own. However, while moral and ethical dilemmas may temporarily appear less black and white as we build our cultural competence, cultural competence does not mean everything is acceptable simply because it's culture. When we are culturally competent, we understand morals and ethics still exist, but they may look quite different when viewed through a different cultural lens.

We learned in Step 5 that treating people the same versus treating them with equity were two different things. The latter requires discernment. Treating all of the students in the example the same way would not be fair. How could the Chinese students know the American definition of "cheating," especially if they're new to the country? What at first glance appeared to be an ethical concern is cultural. Indeed, there should be an expectation they eventually adapt their behavior in the educational setting; however, this adaptation will require learning and time.

Becoming skilled in discernment is key to building cultural competence, but it's not easy to learn. It's much easier to jump to conclusions based on our own experiences and assumptions. It takes time, patience, and a desire to understand ourselves and others. Below are a few steps we can take to become more discerning:

- **Understand context.** We are too quick to punish and too slow to educate. In the current cancel culture environment, many people seem to enjoy punishing people for their mistakes—even some made 20 years ago or more. We argue about Christmas songs and stop publishing books written nearly 90 years ago because we look at them through today's lens of understanding. By no means is racist, sexist, or any behavior that demeans people acceptable. However, we must recognize art forms as representative of the context within which they were created and use objectionable art to educate rather than persecute.

- **Ask yourself: "Is it true, or is it just true for me?"** There is a difference between actual truth and personal truth. Personal truth comes from our experiences, which may or may not align with actual truth. It's human nature to unconsciously assume, "If it's true for me, then it's true for everyone," but that's not the case. We must remember we all have different experiences, leading to our different perspectives.

- **Widen your circle.** We tend to socialize with people who are similar to us, so we have more data to discern both "good" and "bad" people in our group. If a usually good person within our circle of friends does something bad, we recognize it as an anomaly. Maybe they had a bad day. Maybe there were extenuating circumstances we weren't aware of. On the other hand, when we experience or witness someone outside of our group doing something "bad," we have only one data point—the current experience. We don't have the advantage of interacting with that person on a day-to-day basis to understand the context of what happened. It's easy to then look at the entire group as "bad," which simply isn't true. Instead, it's our data that is limited. The more experience we have with people who are different from us in at least one other significant way, the better our data becomes upon which to build context.

A Word About "Culture Fit"

Too often, "culture fit" is used to cover our biases. When someone is deemed not to fit, it's usually a nice way to say, "They're not like us." "Culture fit" implies similar values; however, as we've discovered in this step, similar values do not necessarily imply similar perspectives or behaviors.

A client once said to me, "She's not leadership material! She doesn't speak up in meetings."

I asked my client to elaborate further.

"Well, she's Asian. She's really shy. She's got a lot of good ideas, but I just can't get her to share them in the meeting. I ask her directly for her opinion, and she'll talk a little bit then, but she won't just jump in like everyone else. I want her to succeed, but I don't know how to get her past her shyness."

The first warning light that popped up in my mind was, "She's Asian." That's a huge category, but I was willing to go with it.

I asked my client, "Help me understand why your definition of 'good leader' means people have to speak up in meetings? Are there other ways people can share their ideas and still be a good leader?"

The cultural difference here was between hierarchical and egalitarian cultures. My client was the boss, and when he was in the meeting, his employee would not speak up to ensure he would not lose face. She didn't want to say anything he *should* know because it might mean he was ignorant.

After a bit more discussion, my client decided to meet with his employee before meetings to discuss the agenda and get her input and suggestions. She was much more open with him in their one-on-one meetings, and he could present her ideas in the group.

The idea of "culture fit" should revolve around shared values. In this case, both my client and his employee valued respectful behavior. They were just going about it in different ways. He showed respect by appreciating her input and wanting her voice heard; she showed it by deferring to his role as "boss" in meetings.

Closing out Step 7:
Aligning Values and Behavior

As we've discovered, authenticity doesn't necessarily mean replicating the same behavior everywhere. Instead, it means discerning context within situations and acting in alignment with our values in a way that is appropriate for the context. As a result, we understand *why* we do what we do within those different groups, and we allow our behavior to shift. That's change within context.

This chapter's assignment is to gauge your level of authenticity with respect to your values and determine your most authentic behavior.

- Re-list the values you identified in Step 6. On a scale of 1-5, how authentically do you live this value? Why did you give yourself this rating? How do you become more authentic around this value?

- Go to the online portal at www.TheDWordDiversity.com and download the "Authentic Behaviors Worksheet." In it, you'll find a list of different behaviors and questions to guide you through reflection for your most authentic behavior.

The Strength of Vulnerability

Step 8:

We cultivate the humility to admit we don't know all the answers and to ask the questions we need to ask in order to learn.

An executive once said to me, "You know, Susan, I learned most of what I did about this stuff [cultural competence] by stepping in it."

My answer to him? "Welcome to the club."

We learn best from our mistakes. You can tell your child, "Don't touch the stove! It's hot!" over and over again, but the child doesn't know what "it's hot" means until they touch the stove and burn their hand. After that, you don't need to worry about it.

Everyone is afraid of making mistakes, but we all make them. Think about some of the best lessons you learned in life, and you might discover many of them came about because of a mistake.

Admitting we don't know something can be difficult, especially if we're the leader in an organization or viewed as the expert on a topic. We worry our ignorance will be mocked or equated to not caring. We're so fearful of being wrong that we hold staunchly to our beliefs, even in the face of certain evidence that we are not right. We're more afraid of being wrong than we are of looking foolish.

In the past, vulnerability was considered a weakness. However, we are now learning that vulnerability is a leadership strength.

Diversity Tough Love:

We learn best by making mistakes—and we all make mistakes.

Why Vulnerability Matters

One of the foremost experts on vulnerability, Brené Brown, is quoted as saying, "Vulnerability is not winning or losing; it's having the courage to show up and be seen when we have no control over the outcome. Vulnerability is not weakness; it's our greatest measure of courage."

Vulnerability isn't only about having the courage to let go of our egos and allow our authentic selves to come through; it's also about the ability to admit we're wrong. It means we're okay with our mistakes, and we allow others to make mistakes, too. We have compassion for ourselves when we err, and we have compassion for others when they do.

A typical objection I hear is, "How am I supposed to know everything about every culture?"

You aren't. If you never work with someone from South Africa, you never have to learn anything about South African culture.

However, most of us work with people from another generation or with a different skin color. We have friends and neighbors of different genders and sexual orientations. We might know people of a different religion or economic status at school. We come into contact every day with all of these differences. We must understand that while some of this may not matter to us because it's not part of our identities, it might matter to the people in our lives with these identities. If we care about each other, we should learn about what matters to each other. Vulnerability is about accepting others for whom they are, not who we want them to be.

No one should be expected to know all of the answers, regardless of their role in life. We're vulnerable when we have the humility to admit we don't know all the answers, to ask the questions we need to ask in order to learn, and the discernment to know what to ask.

"Vulnerability, as a resource in leadership and within the workplace, can impact the entire culture and creativity of a team. It can increase output, it can create a place for courage and is a strength that should be harnessed."[1]

Embracing vulnerability means we're willing to learn and grow and change, not because we're bad people, but because we want to be better people.

It's Not Your Fault—Until It Is

At the end of a seminar on unconscious bias, a manager approached me and said, "I'm glad we implemented phone interviews versus in-person interviews."

He told me about interviewing a man for a job opening. The manager thought the applicant had one of the best resumes the manager had ever seen. He was hoping the applicant would interview well, and he did. An offer was extended and accepted.

The manager went to the lobby to welcome his new employee the first day. Upon entering the lobby, the manager saw a man sitting there with long hair pulled back in a ponytail and covered in tattoos. The manager thought. "Oh, boy. I hope that's not my guy!"

He was.

The manager closed his story by saying, "This employee has turned out to be everything I had hoped he would be. He's one of the best hires I've ever made, and if we had interviewed in person, I'm not sure I would have been able to overcome my biases."

This story is one of my favorites because it took self-awareness and vulnerability for the manager to realize his biases and to tell his story. He's been able to overcome some of his own biases about appearance, and he's helped educate others in the organization.

As we learned in Step 3, we start forming our biases even before we're born, and by the time we're seven years old, we operate primarily on autopilot. What can be a little disconcerting is just how young we are when we begin to act on our biases to discern in-groups and out-groups.

Researchers at Yale University's Infant Cognition Center conducted studies to test in-group and out-group dynamics. Babies are asked to choose a treat from a bowl of Cheerios or graham crackers. A puppet play is then performed, and puppets choose treats from the two bowls. When asked which puppet they prefer, babies overwhelmingly gravitate toward the puppet that chose what they did, indicating a preference for those who are "like them."

Then, another puppet play is performed—and this is where things get interesting. Overwhelmingly, babies like good things to happen to the puppets who share their preferences and bad things to happen to the puppets who don't. Researchers say this indicates a preference for "those who are in my group."[2]

If infants as young as seven months old like bad things to happen to the puppets that aren't like them, imagine how ingrained our biases are by the time we reach adulthood. Maybe that helps explain why it's so hard for us to let go of them—because we were born with the beginnings of them, and they are continually shaped and reinforced over many years.

So, how do we become aware of our biases?

One way is to use an online tool called the _Implicit Association Test_ (IAT). The IAT was developed by researchers at Harvard University to help make us aware of our biases. At the time of this writing, there are 14 tests available, and you can test your biases on characteristics like skin tone, religion, and gender identity. For each test, a pair of pictures and words are flashed onto the screen, and you're measured on your response time to each pair. At the end of the test, you're given a brief report letting you know how biased you were in that situation. Notice here that I said, "how biased." I don't want anyone surprised by your results because you will most likely be biased.[3]

Questioning biases that deep can be a bit unnerving. However, only by having the vulnerability to examine our biases can we better understand ourselves. In that understanding, we learn how to reconcile our differences with others.

Asking the Right Questions

I often get asked, "How do I ask people about themselves in a way that's not offensive?" We genuinely want to get things right when talking to others, but we can be so afraid of getting things wrong, we'd rather not ask. We don't see that the assumptions we make about other people based on stereotypes may be a bigger insult.

Until we've mastered Step 6, we unconsciously put ourselves at the center of the universe as a base of comparison for everyone we encounter. As a result, the questions we ask to get to know people tend to highlight how they are "different from me."

Diversity Tough Love:

It's better to be vulnerable and ask a question to learn the answer, rather than assume we know the answer based on a stereotype and risk insult.

An online article, "21 Questions Asian People Are Sick of Answering,"[4] lists questions Asian Americans typically get from majority White people in the United States. Among those questions are:

- "Can you tell the difference between the different types of Asians?"
- "Do you get in trouble if you don't get straight A's?"
- "How are you guys all so skinny?"

I shared the article on social media with my friends. Shortly afterward, a friend of mine who is gay added a few of his own:

- "At what age did you know you were gay?"
- "Do you like to dress in women's clothing?"
- "What do you mean you don't watch 'Will and Grace'?! That show is hilarious!"

Another friend added the Latinx version:

- "Are your parents illegal?"
- "Are you really good at salsa dancing?"
- "Do you play soccer?"

I added my Native American list:

- "Do you smoke a peace pipe?" (Usually followed by, "What do you put in that pipe anyway?")
- "Do you own a teepee?"
- "It hasn't rained in weeks! Can you do a rain dance or something?"

All of these questions come from stereotypes. Stereotypes are broadly applied assumptions that result from limited learning and experience with people from other cultures.

Asking questions of others takes vulnerability, and I genuinely believe these questions come from an attempt to understand people better. Those who ask them are searching to connect and further conversation. Unfortunately, all questions like this do is prove we really don't know each other at all.

A few tips:

- When we ask specific yes/no questions based on an assumption or something we've heard or seen in the media, we're stereotyping.
- Open-ended questions can help us to manage our assumptions better.
- Instead of asking, "Do you eat dog?" try, "What's your favorite cuisine?" Or, instead of, "Do you watch Will and Grace?" try, "What TV shows do you like?"

It's okay to ask questions to get to know each other, but doing so requires self-awareness and some education to know the right questions to ask. If you think this is all just political correctness, it's not. It's being respectful of our fellow humans.

Bouncing Back From Mistakes

We've all said foolish things. How do we best recover?

By building our capacity for resilience.

Why resilience? Well, according to HeartMath®, an organization out of Northern California that has studied resilience for well over 25 years, "resilience is the capacity to prepare for, recover from, and adapt in the face of stress, challenge or adversity."[5] What's unique about this definition is the "prepare for" part. We can practice techniques in advance of stressful times, so we are more at ease when stressors arise.

HeartMath® explains is like this: Imagine you have an internal battery, and resilience is the amount of energy you have stored in that battery. When your battery is fully charged, you can more easily flow through any challenges you encounter. When your battery is rundown, you will have difficulty responding well in challenging situations.

When we learn how to manage our resilience levels, we don't waste unnecessary energy on stressful situations. Instead, we can effectively plug any leaks in our internal battery and build and maintain the energy we need to be more effective in our day-to-day activities.

Building resilience can help us reduce anxiety, improve communication, and boost our performance at work, leading to better business decisions and outcomes. Improved resilience also helps us maintain our composure in challenging situations and self-regulate our emotions, an important part of Step 10.

How can resilience help us to be more vulnerable? In those times where we might not know the answer to a question or are afraid to admit we made a mistake, resilience allows us to reach into ourselves, past the palpitating heart and nervousness, to honestly say, "I don't know," or, "I'm sorry." Resilience can help us with the strength we need to admit we're human and lead with greater compassion.

Too often, we apologize because we want a situation to go away, with little thought as to why we did what we did. We try to distance ourselves from our behavior and come up with excuses rather than own it. However, researchers at Ohio State University found offering an apology helps to repair trust and respect in relationships.[6] Thoughtful apologies contain up to six components, but two of the six components are more important than the others. They are:

- Take ownership; and
- Offer to make amends.

Vulnerability is a two-way street. Responsibility does not just lie with the person who made the mistake. We must be compassionate and allow each other room to learn and grow from our mistakes. If someone says or does something that seems insensitive, don't immediately assume the worst of them. Ask questions and get underneath what happened instead of scolding them for it. Listen when they apologize and try to find it within yourself to accept their apology with grace. After all, that's what you'd want if you were in their shoes, right?

Closing Out Step 8: Practicing Vulnerability

People are messy and complicated beings and getting along with others is not always easy. No matter how hard we try, we're going to mess up occasionally. After all, we're all learning all the time.

Practicing vulnerability takes courage, but it's up to you to take the first step. Below are a few suggestions to get you started. You can find more resources in the portal at www.TheDWordDiversity.com.

Pick one or two of the suggestions below to increase your vulnerability and try to make them a regular practice. If you're just beginning your vulnerability journey, start with the most comfortable suggestions and save more challenging suggestions for when you have more confidence.

- When conversing with a trusted friend or family member, if you don't agree with them, rather than saying nothing, find a way to tell them you don't agree. Or, if they have said something hurtful, let them know.

- Share something about yourself with someone that they might not yet know. It doesn't have to be a big revelation—in fact, smaller is probably better, especially if you are not used to being vulnerable.

- Say, "I don't know, but I'll find out," at least once today. (Make sure to follow up on your promise to find out!)

- Ask for help.

- Play "two truths and a lie" with your family/friends to get to know them better. (Rules: Each person reveals two truths and a lie about themselves. The truths should be relatively unknown to the others in the group. Each person takes a turn reading their statements, and the others have to guess which one is the lie.)

- Reflect on your life or career. What's a big mistake you made? What did you learn from it? Was it truly a big mistake, or did it just seem that way because you were in the middle of it?

Keeping an Open Mind

Step 9:

We maintain nonjudgment and curiosity when we see someone behave differently in word, action, or deed.

I grew up in the desert southwest of the United States. Wildlife to me was roadrunners, quail, snakes, and an occasional scorpion. Those were the things I was used to seeing when I looked out of the window at home, went horseback riding, or drove down the road.

Years later, I was vacationing in Barbados. I was on the back porch of the villa we had rented, and I heard some rustling in the trees next to me. I looked up, but I didn't see anything. The rustling continued. I looked up again, and a monkey came into focus on the outermost branches. Once I saw him, I noticed many others—a mother carrying a baby on the wall right below the tree and two young monkeys running around the base of a tree in the yard next door. I was amazed it took me so long to see the entire family of monkeys right in front of me.

What happened? Well, I did not live in a place where monkeys existed in the wild. I only knew monkeys in the zoo, behind cages, or in beautifully created enclosures. Monkeys were not part of my innate perception of "animals in the wild." As a result, it took me a while before I could perceive the family that was right before me.

We See What We Know

The things we see are the things we expect to see. When something enters our line of sight, and we don't expect it, we might need a minute to focus before we actually see it—or we might not see it at all.

Our cultures influence our perception, and when our perception is influenced, so is our worldview. When we have challenges with other people, we see what our culture has taught us to see, and we believe everyone else sees it just the same way. As we've learned, they don't.

Suppose I gave you this description: "[A] light, flat growth. . . consisting of numerous slender, closely arranged parallel barbs forming a vane on either side of a horny, tapering, partly hollow shaft."[1] Would you know what it is? Certainly, everyone alive has seen one of these—perhaps not up close, but we've all seen one.

If I told you that you could find these growths on birds, you would realize the description is of a feather.

We give things their meaning. If I were to hand you a pencil, you would know its purpose is to write. You know that because you've been taught that, and you've used pencils. You give it meaning through what you've been taught and your own experiences. Even just saying "pencil" gives you a mental image. How would you describe a pencil? Both you and a friend might describe it differently, but you both would share the meaning of "pencil."

Suppose I asked you to describe a utensil for eating. If you grew up in a place that used forks, knives, and spoons, you would describe those. On the other hand, if you grew up in China, Japan, or Korea, you would describe chopsticks. Depending on the community in which you grew up and what type of utensils your family used, you may be even more specific about the type of material used in fashioning the utensils.

Our culturally ingrained knowledge teaches us the meaning of things. It's what we're brought up with and how we share meaning with those we know. We work from our frame of reference because, too often, it's the only frame we have. If you grew up in a place with forks and were dropped into a place with chopsticks, you might not even know what a chopstick was, much less how to use it. It would take inquiry, observation, and practice.

Understanding the meaning around pencils and eating utensils is just a start to understanding how we create meaning based on our culture. We often don't realize that what we learn and observe from our families and communities is not the same thing others learn and observe. We may write a person off as rude, racist, or untrustworthy because of one interaction, but, as we learned in Step 7, we must consider context and discern if our assumptions are accurate. It was likely just one or two behaviors that resulted in our negative judgment. Perhaps, the person was having a bad day. Maybe you were having a bad day. While rude people exist, it's more likely good people exhibit rude behavior. When making value judgments, it's essential to step back and understand our way is not the only way.

Language is an essential part of creating meaning. A different word might be used for the same object, yet we share the same meaning. I'd use *el tenedor* if I were in a Spanish-speaking country or *la fourchette* in France, yet I'd still use the fork the same way.

The language we speak changes our brains and our perspectives. It engrains in us a particular view of the world and plays a significant role in how we construct reality. Researchers have found Russian speakers can better differentiate different shades of blue because the Russian language distinguishes between dark and light shades of blue. Speakers of languages that do not have as differentiated a language *do not physically see certain shades*. Imagine arguing over who is right and who is wrong about what shade of blue the sky is when each individual is correct based on their own knowledge! Instead, it's easier to understand different languages contain different worldviews, and if we learn a new language, we also incorporate new perspectives and new ways to see the world.[2]

There is never *only one* perspective for anything. Electricity can be helpful, or it can kill. Medicine can make us healthy or sick. A table can be used as a chair, and vice versa. When two people look at the same thing, there are two perspectives of the same thing. We might agree a table is a table, but how we describe or use the table might be very different.

How Do We Know Things?

I think of knowledge in two ways: personal knowledge and universal knowledge. Personal knowledge is an individual's understanding of the world. It is what we have learned throughout our life, and it is the information we use daily to make judgments and decisions. Personal knowledge continually evolves based on our education and experience. Presented with new information, we have a choice to accept it or not.

The universal pool of knowledge is the store of information to which we all have access. It is the knowledge that simply exists. Just because we are not aware of a particular piece of knowledge does not mean it doesn't exist. A "discovery" is merely finding something that was always there. If it weren't, we wouldn't have found it. For example, doctors use their detailed medical knowledge daily. I am not a doctor, nor do I have much medical knowledge, but that does not negate the fact medical knowledge exists. Yogis can control their breathing and meditate for hours on end. Just because I cannot do it does not mean the knowledge to do so doesn't exist. If I wanted to study to become a doctor or a yogi, I would need to activate different types of knowledge. Knowledge exists; learning is a choice.

We are continuously giving meaning to the things in our world. Sometimes, our meaning doesn't make sense when we look at it through another lens. If you were in a room with only 23 people, what would be your intuitive guess that two people sitting in that room had the same birthday? When we consider there are 365 days in the year, it makes intuitive sense that, in a room of 23 people, it's pretty unlikely two people have the same birthday. However, using probability theory, we can prove there's a 50/50 chance two people in a room of 23 have the same birthday. In fact, all we need is 70 people in the room to get over a 99% chance. Accurate information doesn't always make intuitive sense, so it can be easy to dismiss.

While a discovery is finding something that was already there, it's also true that just because we haven't discovered something yet doesn't mean it doesn't exist. We tend to discount the experiences of other people because "it didn't happen to me." I have a friend who has been diagnosed as bipolar. I used to try to discern whether the story they were telling was "real" or not—until I realized it didn't matter if it was *real to me*. The experience was *real to them*, and it contributed to their perspective. It is never our place to negate another's experience.

Sometimes Random Doesn't Look so Random

Every leader I've spoken to says they want the best person for the job. We know gender diversity on teams can increase the organization's dollar value by millions, and racially diverse teams are more creative and innovative.[3] If talent is equally distributed, we would expect visible representation within organizations to look roughly like the local population across all organizational levels. We strive for diversity based on optics.

One of my clients, a woman banking executive, said to me, "I got into my last board meeting, and I looked around. It was all women! We were so proud of ourselves! Not one man in sight."

While I've been working in the D&I field for over 20 years, my formal education is in mathematics. I have a Master of Science degree in Statistics. (Hence, the birthday statistics problem above.) I love numbers and solving problems, and if you ever have a coaching session with me, you'll likely have to endure some math examples.

As a statistician, I know sometimes you can flip a coin ten times and get "heads" every time. Are ten "heads" likely? No, but it *is* possible.

Is it possible an all-woman Board of Directors has the best local talent for the job? Yes, it's possible.

Is it likely? No.

Diversity Tough Love:

Optics isn't the best way to ensure diversity.
A team that looks "diverse" may not be "diverse."

When we focus on optics, not only do we diminish the diversity we can't see—things like neurodiversity, economic background, military experience, etc.—we run the risk of thinking an overcorrection means we have achieved equity. However, overcorrection is not the answer if we still don't have the best people for the jobs.

No matter what the optics are, questioning the numbers requires open-mindedness. A team that looks diverse may not be, and a team that looks the same could be. In either case, the only way we can be confident of the answer is if we have mastered The 12 Steps to Diversity Recovery™ and built solid processes and procedures.

Thinking with an Open Mind

Not everyone naturally has an open mind, but we can all develop one by being aware of how we react to new ideas, people, and situations. Do we choose to shut them down, wall them off, and avoid them? Or do we ask questions, get curious, and engage?

As we've learned, our brains are wired to make judgments. Some of the judgments we make are necessary for our survival—like fleeing a burning house. However, many of our judgments come from our own biases, fears, and inexperience. We must make it a priority to withhold judgment in situations that are not life or death situations, even when it goes against every fiber of our being.

When we are open-minded, we are:

- Willing to see things from other perspectives even if we disagree with them.
- Open to feedback when we see the world with tunnel vision and are receptive to new ideas.
- Able to withhold judgment from the differences we face and desire to learn and engage with others in new ways.

Having an open mind means we hold space for other ways of being, and we respect and acknowledge there are ways of moving in the world that are just as nuanced and complex as our own, even if we don't fully understand them.

Finally, be deliberate in seeking out other perspectives as much as you can—not just when you're trying to solve a problem, but also when you're building a team or considering someone for hire or promotion. The more perspectives you learn, the more innovative and open you can be.

Closing out Step 9:
Make understanding new perspectives a habit in your daily life.

Keeping an open mind goes against our nature. New experiences can seem threatening because they are unfamiliar, and our brain registers them as threats. We ignore statistics because of personal experience. We think, "That can't be true! I've never had that happen to me."

Below are a few easy ways to start practicing open-mindedness:

1. When you find yourself judging something too harshly today, first stop and ask yourself: Why? What is this person mirroring back to me? What is the lesson I have to learn about this situation? (You can review the concept of "mirroring" in Step 6.)

2. Start to get curious instead of judgmental. Become a reporter and ask questions to understand the complete picture of what's going on. Here are three ideas to get you started (Go back to Step 8 for more ideas):
   - "What did you mean by that?"
   - "Help me understand your perspective."
   - "Tell me more about that."

3. Listen. Be open to what the other person is saying. Make an effort to get into their shoes and understand it from their perspective. Try not to come up with counterpoints to prove them wrong. Instead, be willing to share your perspective nondefensively. Also, realize you may have to agree to disagree.

Be sure to go to the portal at www.TheDWordDiversity.com for more ideas on how you can further develop an open mind.

Your Emotional Guidance System

Step 10:

We notice when we feel good, we are in alignment with our beliefs, values, and expectations.
When we don't feel good, we aren't in alignment.

In Step 3, we learned we share values, but we have different expressions of those values.

Let's take a deeper look at the value of "respect."

Everyone wants to be respected. I was raised by a father who said, "Look at me when I'm talking to you!" I was taught that eye contact is respectful behavior—it shows I'm paying attention to the person speaking.

Now suppose I'm interviewing someone for a job who is not making eye contact with me. I may think they're shy, or they're not paying attention, or they're dishonest. I don't feel very good about the person's behavior, no matter what I believe. In fact, I feel pretty annoyed, and I think to myself, "This person isn't respectful, and we value respect here. They aren't going to be a good fit for our culture." As a result, I don't offer them the job. Instead, I offer the job to the person who made eye contact in the interview because my brain registered the expected behavior. I felt connected to the person because their behavior indicated they were listening to me, and, therefore, they were respectful.

However, there are cultures where no eye contact is considered respectful behavior. The interviewee who did not make eye contact might have been disrespectful, or they might have been expressing respect, but in a way I was not familiar with. I may have just dismissed a potentially excellent employee because their behavior for the same value was at odds with what I was taught.

How do we slow down our thinking so we're not jumping to conclusions, and we can discover whether what we're witnessing is disrespect or culture?

By paying attention to our emotions.

Our Bridge to Awareness

Emotional intelligence is a key component to connecting to ourselves. Our emotions are our internal guidance system. They let us know when things are going along according to our beliefs, values, and expectations and when they are not. If you're happy, it means what's happening aligns with your beliefs, values, and expectations. If you're angry, it means it doesn't. It's that simple.

We accept information we feel good about because it confirms our beliefs, and we reject information that makes us feel bad because it conflicts with our beliefs. If something makes us feel bad, we seek relief by looking for information that makes us feel better. This is how confirmation bias is formed.

For instance, let's take the hot topic of climate change. Many have the opinion climate change is tied to a political agenda. Their belief about climate change depends on the information presented by the political party they support. If they are presented with conflicting information, they get angry because it does not align with their beliefs. They gravitate towards theories that align with their beliefs because it makes them feel better.

The key is to be aware of our emotions and understand how they influence our beliefs. Are our feelings of skepticism or control or fear keeping us from furthering our understanding of a situation? If so, it may be important to back away from those feelings and re-examine the situation from a different perspective. We will never change our beliefs unless our feelings change first.

The bridge to understanding ourselves and others is built by our emotions.

Pay attention to your emotional reaction in situations. It's easy to accept unimportant information if you have a positive reaction and discount essential information if you have a negative emotional reaction. When we understand our emotional reactions and use them to discern the beliefs that are being supported or challenged, we can more accurately determine what we need to do to resolve our situation.

Emotional intelligence isn't just about understanding our own emotions. It plays a key role in building empathy and understanding for others. When we are emotionally intelligent, we can connect with others on a different level. We understand their smiles may not be authentic, or their gratitude may just be a way to make *us* feel better. We understand tears of joy may have behind them tears of fear and inadequacy.

The Internet, Empathy, and Cultural Competence

Researchers have looked at how the internet affects our brains and may be killing empathy.[1] The internet has become so embedded in our lives in North America (over 90% of the population uses it[2]) that browsing, social networking, and watching videos are daily occurrences. Children have become incredibly adept at multi-tasking and amassing vast amounts of time using technology and watching videos. All of this time can lead to desensitization and a lack of ability to develop empathy.

There is a general feeling today's kids "get it" in terms of diversity. Younger generations have been exposed to more differences at earlier ages. They seem more tolerant and understanding of people than even those just one generation ahead of them. However, empathy is a critical skill in building cultural competence. Empathy helps us shift our thinking, see things from other perspectives, and imagine thoughts and feelings from another person's point of view. Having empathy involves understanding others' beliefs and desires and recognizing facial expressions and the feelings those expressions may be linked to. If using the internet is causing us to become desensitized to other people's emotions, it won't be easy to develop cultural competence.

The COVID-19 pandemic forced companies to move to remote work wherever possible. Teams no longer sat next to each other in the same office, and communication was relegated to messaging applications and video meetings. This way of working is unlikely to go away, as companies and employees realize the cost savings.[3] Being physically disconnected will require us to find new ways to emotionally connect with one another to foster empathy and build cultural competence. A study conducted at Barrett Values Center found "employees are asking for even more communication, innovation, and collaborative ways of working together" as a way forward.[4]

Emotions and Our Beliefs About Equity

Diversity Tough Love:

Not everyone has the same shot at succeeding, regardless of how hard they work.

In response to the latest racist attack in the news, I often see posts from White friends on social media with pictures of White and Black children holding hands. My friends will say, "See! They're colorblind. Racism is taught," or, "One race. The human race."

What they don't realize is being colorblind is a privilege. Talking about race issues is uncomfortable for them because it goes against their belief of "We're all equal." It's uncomfortable when we realize we're not all treated that way.

The odds are stacked against some more than others. One study[5] found Black men had to have more education than White men to get the same job. Another study[6] found job applicants with "White sounding" names were more likely to get job callbacks than those with "Black sounding" names. Wage gaps persist by gender and race.[7] (There are probably at least 100 more studies I could find that show everyone doesn't have the same opportunity for success, but I'll leave that as homework for you.)

I think, too often, people feel there's someone who needs to be blamed for the inequities. Others feel guilt. Still others are afraid if they admit there's bias in the system, the scales will somehow suddenly shift the other way, and they will lose the power and privilege that's benefited them for so long.

The truth is, none of this should, or will, happen. The only blame to be placed, and guilt to be felt, is if we don't open our eyes and become part of the solution. The scales of inequity won't tip overnight, if ever. In fact, it's a bit hypocritical to claim belief in equality and, at the same time, be afraid to lose your privileges.

If we recognize we're having a strong emotional reaction to certain news, we can question the belief it's bumping up against. Then, we can decide whether or not we want to investigate that belief. The more informed we are about a situation and the more open we are to different perspectives, the more likely we are to come to better conclusions.

- When we're colorblind, we believe justice serves everyone. When we see color, we understand it does not.

- When we're colorblind, we believe everyone is treated the same. When we see color, we see everyone is not.

- When we're colorblind, we believe everyone has the same opportunities in life. When we see color, we understand some people may not have access to certain opportunities, or if they do, they may have to work harder for the same opportunities.

I encourage everyone to understand the deeper issues around systemic racism rather than just looking at individual incidences on the surface. We all believe we're good people, and I honestly believe the great majority of us are. Try finding the common humanity. We all want to be respected. We all want to be loved. We all want to be safe.

Then, start seeing color and ask yourself, "Are we all respected? Are we all loved? Are we all safe?"

I think you might be surprised at the answers.

(If you're having an emotional reaction reading this, I invite you to figure out what belief got stepped on as you were reading it.)

Shifting Your Perspective in the Heat of a Disagreement

Our emotions are the primary driver of our physiology. How we feel at any given moment affects our heart rhythm, which in turn affects our brain. Emotions such as anger, frustration, and fear can create irregular and incoherent heart rate rhythms, which interfere with our ability to think clearly.[8]

When we aren't resilient, we typically don't respond kindly. We can get frustrated more easily and say things we later regret.

When we have built up our capacity for resilience, we can adapt more quickly. Little things don't seem to bother us as much. We practice shifting our emotions to gratitude, appreciation, and care, creating more harmonious heart rhythms and a clearer mind. When our minds are clear, we think more freely and respond more favorably, even in challenging situations.

We all know how easy it is to make one comment to someone, whether it's in person or on social media, and quickly find ourselves in a heated argument. We get caught up in trying to convince others we're right, and we get offended when their opinions are different than ours. We end up frustrated, angry, and misunderstood.

We may not feel like we have any control over these conversations, but we do. Now that you've found yourself in a tug-o'-war conversation, what can you do?

First, step away. If you're on social media, get off. If you're in person, feel free to say, "I'm not comfortable with where this conversation is going. Can we just end it?" or a simple, "I don't want to discuss this anymore." You don't have to give a reason. If being direct makes you feel uncomfortable, excuse yourself to the bathroom or to get a drink of water. Whatever it takes, remove yourself from the situation.

Second, notice your feelings. If you're feeling aggravated or angry, what belief or value of yours is being triggered? Understanding this can help you redirect the conversation. For instance, if you notice your belief about "respect" is being challenged, you can say, "Can we agree everyone wants to be treated with respect?" From this base of common agreement, you have two options: 1) End the conversation with the agreement; or 2) Build on the agreement to understand how each of you is defining "respectful behavior" differently.

Third, use mirroring. Mirroring can help us understand our emotions, and it can also help us understand others. When someone is calling us angry, we can use mirroring to recognize what they see is their own anger, which can help us not take their words personally. It can also help us build empathy as we try to understand why they are angry. (If you need to review mirroring, see Step 6.)

Finally, refocus your attention. When we're frustrated or angry, we often do not think straight. To calm ourselves down and clear up the pathway between our heart and our brain, we need to refocus our attention. There are a couple of easy ways to do this.

If you have stepped away from the conversation, pull up a picture of someone or something you love. Anything that gives you a feeling of calm, comfort, or love in your heart will do. Take a few moments to focus your attention on that picture to draw your attention away from the discussion and refocus on a more peaceful topic.

If you're in the middle of an argument, you can try the Quick Coherence® Technique from HeartMath. This technique may be something you already naturally do, maybe even without knowing it. Your goal with Quick Coherence is to use your heart to balance your thoughts and emotions.

> "Step 1: Focus your attention in the area of the heart. Imagine your breath is flowing in and out of your heart or chest area, breathing a little slower and deeper than usual.
>
> "Step 2: Make a sincere attempt to experience a regenerative feeling such as appreciation or care for someone or something in your life."[9]

With this technique, it should only take a minute or two to gain a more balanced and coherent state.

Closing out step 10:
Connecting to Your Emotional Guidance System

We can't develop our emotional guidance system without awareness, authenticity, vulnerability, and open-mindedness, so it's time to engage all the lessons you've learned up to now.

In the exercises for Steps 1, 6, and 7, we learned more about our values and beliefs. Before jumping into the exercises for Step 10, take a few minutes to review your work in those steps.

1. Over the next day, pay attention to your initial reaction to other people's behavior. If you are feeling calm or happy, how are your values being reflected in the situation? If you feel frustrated or angry, how are your values not being reflected in the situation?

2. Review the "Authentic Behaviors Worksheet" from Step 7, and think about your authentic behaviors. (You can find the worksheet in the portal at www.TheDWordDiversity.com.) How do you feel when someone acts like you? When they don't?

3. How does connecting to your feelings help you become aware of your preferences, expectations, beliefs, and values?

4. How can you use your emotional intelligence to connect to others and become more aware, authentic, vulnerable, and open-minded in the future?

Compassionate Diversity®

Step 11:

We remember learning about ourselves and others often happens through making mistakes.
We grant ourselves and others grace when we mess up.

A friend of mine at university was paralyzed after a skydiving accident. In the years after his accident, he learned how to live a new, independent life from his wheelchair. He even had a customized van and drove himself around town, which those of us who were first-year students envied because we weren't allowed to have cars.

One day, I was walking to class with him. His wheelchair hit a bump on the pathway, and the book he had sitting in his lap fell to the ground. I rushed to pick it up, but he said to me, "Susan, will you let me do that? I'm perfectly capable of picking up my own book."

I was a bit shocked because I only wanted to be helpful. I certainly didn't intend to imply he was incapable; I already knew he could physically do just about everything I could with little to no modification. While he appreciated my intent to be helpful, he absolutely could pick up the book himself. Picking up a book seemed helpful to me, and it was something

I would do for anyone. For my friend, picking up a book represented his independence.

Many of us want to help when we see people struggling, and sometimes we jump right in before asking if they even want to be helped. We help from our perspective of what we think we would want in their position—we treat them as we would want to be treated. We grab control of the situation in an attempt to ease our discomfort without considering the other person might be perfectly comfortable with what's happening.

To build more trust in our relationships, we must allow room for others to be different from us and allow people to define what they need, not give them what we think they need. Sometimes, the best action is to let go.

Letting go doesn't mean we don't do things for other people; rather, it means we slow down and check our biases before acting. We let go of our preconceived notions and long-held beliefs or ways of doing things. We ask before we act. When we don't ask, we're unconsciously using our privilege to usurp control from others, and we imply our way is the better way to do things. It may be better for us, but it doesn't mean it's better for everyone.

Diversity Tough Love:

Helping others may be a way to relieve your own discomfort in situations and assert your privilege.

A New Approach to Diversity & Inclusion[3]

While there have been a few adjustments here and there, we tend to teach diversity and inclusion the same way we did years ago—through logic

---

[3] Large portions of this section are reprinted with permission from my chapter, "Five Ways to Bring Compassion into Your Organization," published in: Mongan, M. (Ed.). (2018). *Brilliant Breakthroughs for the Small Business Owner: Fresh Perspectives on Profitability, People, Productivity, and Finding Peace in Your Business.²*

and facts. There have been a lot of articles written about why diversity training doesn't work, but after over 20 years in this field, I know why:

- First, we force people through classes that pile on guilt for some while leaving others feeling justified.
- Second, we don't teach a subject that is all *about people* in a way that actually *connects with* people. We teach to the head and not to the heart.
- Third, we fail to make connections for people about the personal benefits of things like self-awareness and understanding others.

Diversity Tough Love:

We've been doing diversity work the same way for too long with few tangible results.

Today, more and more leadership research is focused on areas like authenticity, vulnerability, and mindfulness. There is a growing acknowledgment, both inside and outside of business, of the need to connect with different people and perspectives in more meaningful ways. One way we can do this is through developing compassion.

Compassion does not excuse the historic and systemic injustices in society. In fact, compassion demands even more effort than the old, worn diversity path that hasn't worked for years because it requires us to actually take time to understand how these injustices affect everyone *from their perspective.* Reaching this point is a step-by-step journey, calling for not only deep introspection but also an ability to recognize injustices, to understand different perspectives, and to step into another person's shoes in a respectful, curious, caring way.

In Step 2, we discussed the personal benefits of compassion, and there are also benefits for business.

- First, compassion within businesses relieves stress and burnout.[2] Stress at work not only affects our health, but it can also affect our work relationships and focus, too.[3] Researchers find that giving and receiving compassion in the workplace decreases depression and negative feelings—like irritability and aggression—and increases creativity, performance, and productivity. People miss less work due to illness, which decreases health care expenses.

- Second, compassion increases a sense of community. Compassion deepens connections to the organization and each other.[4] When we care about each other and the work we do, we build better relationships at work, which leads to more commitment to the workplace. The end result is lower turnover and higher productivity and engagement.[5]

- Third, compassion leads to better financial results.[6] By now, this should be obvious. We all know the results of compassion outlined above—fewer absences, lower healthcare costs, decreased turnover, and higher productivity—lead to better financial results.

Compassion is proven science. The more we experience it in the workplace, the more likely we are to pass it on to others, increasing connection and belonging—and, in turn, more inclusive workplaces.

The Road to Compassion

The path to compassion runs through the Compassionate Diversity® Solution Process we introduced as a discussion model in Step 4. Fundamental to this approach are the 3 C's: Comprehension, Connection, and Collaboration.

At the Comprehension level, we can sympathize with others, but that's about it. We can understand what they are going through, but we tend to lack any deeper connection. We have the best of intentions, but, at this level, we tend to understand the issue only from our own perspective.

At the Connection level, we can begin to empathize. We understand, and we connect to experiences we have had. We begin to relate to the feelings of others, and, as a result, enhance connection. In our efforts to connect, we tend to project our experiences on the other. We assume their situation is just like ours. But it isn't. As a result, we may leave the other person feeling robbed of their experience or misunderstood.

Collaboration is using Comprehension and Connection to act in more compassionate ways. Through Collaboration, we can see from, value, and integrate others' perspectives. We create more compassionate environments. We can develop more innovative and sustainable solutions in our communities and our organizations.

The story of Greg Smith and Amy Jo[7] illustrates how powerful this approach is.

Both Greg and Amy Jo lived in Orlando. Amy Jo was homeless, and Greg passed her on the street every day on his way to work. Greg introduced himself, and they started meeting for monthly lunches. Over the course of their lunches, Greg learned Amy Jo's biggest issue wasn't hunger. It was that she couldn't read, so Greg taught her to read.

Here's how the 3C's connect to Greg and Amy Jo:

- First, Comprehension. When Greg met Amy Jo, he had his own idea about what it meant to be homeless, just like we all do. We can imagine what we would feel like if we were homeless. We probably think money or hunger would be our biggest issue.

- Next, Connection. Greg connected to Amy Jo's positive attitude, and he introduced himself. He invited her out to lunch, and they started meeting monthly. At this level, we tend to project our ideas of what's important onto the homeless folks we see, and we give them money or food. But, as we continue building Comprehension and Connection, we discover what *we* think is important may not be so important to the other person.

- Finally, Collaboration. As trust grew, Greg learned the truth from Amy Jo. She had access to food at a nearby shelter. Her issue was that she couldn't read—and that's a detriment to finding a job. Greg had to let go of his initial assumption that Amy Jo was hungry and shift to help her in a way that was more meaningful to her.

When we find compassion, we understand what is essential to others *from their perspective*. And then we act on that understanding to affect deeper, more meaningful change.

Yes, Forgiveness is Necessary

I'm curious—do you let situations repeatedly play in your head?

Have you thought, "Oh! I should have said *that*!"

Or wondered, "Why was that person so mean?"

We *choose* to let situations live on in our heads. When we hold onto old beliefs, ideas, or behaviors, we don't have room for anything new to enter our lives. Think of it like a closet. If it's stuffed full of clothes, there's no place to hang anything new. When we focus on past events, we are continually recreating the event. If we want to create more compassion in our lives, we must learn to let go of things that no longer serve us. In many situations, we must let go of our idea about how things "should" be and recognize there is seldom just one correct answer. When we release our need to be right, we release judging ourselves, and we can be more kind to ourselves and others.

Perhaps the most important thing we have to learn to let go of is when we think others have wronged us. The best way we can do that is through forgiveness.

Before we go any further, let's clear up a few of the fallacies about forgiveness. First, forgiveness is not about absolution or letting someone off the hook for doing something wrong, nor does it mean they have our permission to have acted in the way they did. Forgiveness doesn't necessarily mean we have to forget what happened; sometimes, it's important *not* to forget, so we don't repeat our mistakes. Forgiveness is not something we do for others.

Forgiveness is something we do for ourselves.

Anger can have detrimental effects beyond just our emotional well-being. Have you ever been so angry you couldn't think straight? If so, it's because your body is reacting to the situation by flooding it with stress chemicals in response to what's happening and cutting off the connection between your brain and heart.[8] Moreover, it's not just the initial event that affects us. When we play situations repeatedly in our heads, the event is replayed in our bodies, too. With every replay comes a release of more stress chemicals. When we can learn to let go through forgiveness, we may develop healthier bodies, too.

When we learn to become more resilient, we practice shifting from emotions that aren't helpful for our mind, body, and spirit and find ones that are. The more we practice letting go of draining emotions, the more we build our capacity for resilience. In turn, the more resilient we become, the better able we are to adapt and shift perspectives in different situations, allowing us to let go of the things that no longer serve us. We can pause into moments of deeper discernment and make more thoughtful decisions.

We allow room for healing when we grant space for different perspectives to coexist. For example, we've learned we all value respect, but we show it in different ways. When all involved understand those ways, we shift to a deeper understanding of respect *and* develop appreciation. Appreciation is a heart-based emotion that can help us build resilience.

More than anything else, forgiveness is a way to show compassion for ourselves. Forgiveness:

- allows us to let go of perceived wrongs;
- gives our minds and bodies space to recover; and
- helps us refocus on more positive things so we can build our energy up again.

All situations require us to release something—even the choice to act means we've let go of the choice not to act. Forgiveness is necessary to release negative thoughts and conditions, but it takes time and patience. It's not something we arrive at overnight, but when we get there, we realize it's the best thing we could do—for ourselves.

Closing out Step 11:
Increasing Compassion by Letting Go

Step 8 addressed vulnerability; we all make mistakes. After we acknowledge our errors (or maybe had them pointed out to us), we must work through Steps 9 and 10 before being able to let go of the things that no longer serve us. Letting go is an act of self-compassion.

1. Think about the values, beliefs, behaviors, and emotions you've reviewed in The 12 Steps to Diversity Recovery™ so far. What are you most rigid about? Why? Can you benefit from letting go of some rigidity? (Note: You don't have to let go of your values, beliefs, and behaviors, but you do have to let go of your expectations about the values, beliefs, and behaviors of others and the idea that we all value, believe, and behave the same way.)

2. Find examples of things you have already let go of by examining how your values, beliefs, and behaviors have changed through the years. Did you reprioritize your values? Did you learn new or more effective behaviors? Did your belief about a particular topic shift? Why? What led to the change?

3. Think of a situation that is a challenge for you right now. What do you need to let go of to ease the challenge? How can you become more compassionate with yourself and others by letting things be?

Don't forget to head out to the portal at www.TheDWordDiversity.com for more ideas about compassion, letting go, and forgiveness.

Never Stop Learning

Step 12:

We know learning is a lifelong journey.
We commit to taking the necessary time to build better connections in all
our relationships.

I grew up an airline brat. My mother worked for a major airline, and from the time I was eight years old, going on vacation meant getting on an airplane. I've been to Hawaii so many times I can't count them all. I spent a three-day school weekend in Brussels, Belgium. When my sister and I were both taking French lessons in school, our Christmas present was a trip to Paris.

My mom never wanted us to take the privilege of hopping on a plane for granted, so she turned every trip into a learning opportunity. When we went to France, we were expected to speak French. The Brussels trip meant asking my Social Studies teacher if I could write a report about my trip for extra credit. It didn't matter if we had been to a place before or not—every time we went to Hawaii, we had to learn or do something new.

My mother instilled in me a love of learning.

Theory and reality are two different things. Learning alone—reading a book, seeing a movie, sitting in a lecture—isn't enough. We have to reinforce what we learn through our experiences. That's how school works: learn something, do some exercises, make mistakes, try again. It's what I've worked to develop throughout this book.

We must practice if we want to keep our skills. I was fluent enough in French during our trip to Paris to have conversations with the locals. I haven't practiced speaking French in years. I still know a few phrases, but I certainly would not be able to get around Paris as easily as I did then.

Learn, Unlearn, Relearn

"The illiterate of the 21st century will not be those who cannot read and write, but those who cannot learn, unlearn, and relearn."

– Alvin Toffler

Building cultural competence requires learning, unlearning, and relearning.

We learn about ourselves and how the people around us influence our worldviews. Then, we learn about and experience different ways of being. We might have grown up with a friend from a different religion. We went to their house and discovered they do things differently. They ate different food, said different prayers. As we learned in Step 10, when we run into behavior different from our own, we may, at first, feel confused or curious or frustrated or excited. We must discern why we're feeling what we're feeling about the behavior. We need to figure out what that new behavior represents. Is it a different value or a different interpretation of a similar value? Depending on the answer, we may need to unlearn our interpretation of the behavior and relearn a new interpretation.

Conflicting information creates discomfort because it doesn't fit into the habits of thinking we've formed over the years. We want to dismiss it and find other information that conforms to our current way of thinking. However, ignoring different information causes us to remain stagnant and become rigid. We are not flexible enough to understand that the way we see the world is not the only way to see the world. From this perspective, we view the world in terms of duality and absolutes, which leads to limited "I'm right/You're wrong" thinking.

In order to unlearn and relearn, we need to make room for both/and thinking. We develop both/and thinking through our learning and experiences. The more we learn and experience, the more expanded our perspectives become, and we can draw upon these perspectives when we encounter challenging situations. We have more possibilities for creating meaning (Step 9), and we develop better discernment (Step 7). As a result, we develop more innovative and sustainable solutions, the very definition of cultural competence.

Life is not black and white. There is a lot of gray. When we are willing to unlearn and relearn, when we can hold space for both/and thinking, we can navigate the gray *and* learn to see all the beautiful colors in between.

Our Journey Together

Suppose you and I are going on a vacation together. You decide to drive, and I take an airplane. When we arrive, we talk about our travels. You describe the twisting roads and the flatlands, the quaint town where you stopped for gas, and the rainstorm that slowed down traffic. I talk about the harried security officers, the relatively smooth flight, and the sun shining above the clouds. We both had very different experiences, yet we are now in the same place.

It's the same way with life. We all have different paths, but we come together for moments in time, whether at school or work or a local community function. What brought us together creates shared meaning, but the stories about *how* we got there differ for each of us. It's in the *how* where diversity lies, and it's in understanding each other's *how* that we create more connected and authentic relationships.

Completing this book doesn't mean you're done. You've only just begun. Building cultural competence and practicing Compassionate Diversity® are life-long learning process.

- You will always discover more about yourself and the world around you, and with each discovery, you will add a new perspective to how you see the world.

- You will always encounter new people and new situations, and with each encounter, you will learn more effective behavior for connecting with others.

- You will always run into challenges, and with each challenge, you will add to your repertoire of solutions and develop new ways to become more compassionate.

Continuous learning means we are engaged with life and with others. We are committed to valuing our similarities and celebrating our differences. We are committed to understanding each other and making our world more meaningful. We are committed to living in a world with more compassion.

Make the commitment today.

Closing Out Step 12:
Commit to Continuous Learning

Commit to continuous learning. Practice what you've learned through this book. Re-visit it and reflect:

- Where could you use more work?

- What do you need to understand more about yourself or others?

- What one thing can you commit to each week to move your journey forward? Put a reminder on your calendar. Ask a friend for help.

Check-in at the portal, www.TheDWordDiversity.com, for more tools and resources to guide your continued learning around cultural competence and Compassionate Diversity®.

Enjoy your journey!

References

Beginning the Conversation

1. Yam, K. (2021, March 9). *Anti-Asian Hate Crimes Increased by Nearly 150% in 2020, Mostly in N.Y. and L.A., New Report Says.* NBCNews. com. https://www.nbcnews.com/news/asian-america/anti-asian-hate-crimes-increased-nearly-150-2020-mostly-n-n1260264.

2. National Congress of American Indians. (2018, February). *Research Policy Update: Violence Against American Indian and Alaska Native Women.* https://www.ncai.org/policy-research-center/research-data/prc-publications/VAWA_Data_Brief__FINAL_2_1_2018.pdf 3.

3. Centers for Disease Control and Prevention. (2021, April 23). *Risk for COVID-19 Infection, Hospitalization, and Death By Race/Ethnicity.* Centers for Disease Control and Prevention. https://www.cdc.gov/coronavirus/2019-ncov/covid-data/investigations-discovery/hospi-talization-death-by-race-ethnicity.html.

4. DiTrolio, M. (2021, January 8). *140,000 Jobs Were Lost in December. All Were Held by Women.* Yahoo! Finance. https://finance.yahoo.com/amphtml/finance/news/140-000-jobs-were-lost-003400030.html.

5. Ford, R. T. (2020, August 18). *Opinion: There is no 'White culture'.* CNN. https://www.cnn.com/2020/08/18/opinions/american-culture-and-race-ford/index.html.

Us vs. Them

1. Emamzadeh, A. (2019, August 09). *The Psychology of "Us-vs-Them".* Psychology Today. https://www.psychologytoday.com/us/blog/finding-new-home/201908/the-psychology-us-vs-them.

2. ScienceDaily. (2014, February 27). *The Pain of Social Exclusion: Physical Pain Brain Circuits Activated by 'Social Pain'.* ScienceDaily. https://www.sciencedaily.com/releases/2014/02/140227101125.htm.

3. Hanson, R. (2019, August 27). *Confronting the Negativity Bias.* Dr. Rick Hanson. https://www.rickhanson.net/how-your-brain-makes-you-easily-intimidated/.

4. Hoffman, A. (2015, June 26). *Can Negative Thinking Make You Sick?* Health.com. https://www.health.com/condition/heart-disease/can-negative-thinking-make-you-sick.

5. Walford, M. (2017, July 28). *Stress: It's Not in Your Head, it's in Your Nervous System.* UPLIFT. https://upliftconnect.com/stress-its-not-in-your-head-its-in-your-nervous-system/.

6. Silverstein, J. (2013, March 11). *How Racism is Bad for Our Bodies.* The Atlantic. https://www.theatlantic.com/health/archive/2013/03/how-racism-is-bad-for-our-bodies/273911/.

7. Barnes, L., De Leon, C., Lewis, T., Bienias, J., Wilson, R., & Evans, D. (2008, July). *Perceived Discrimination and Mortality in a Population-Based Study of Older Adults.* American Journal of Public Health. https://www.ncbi.nlm.nih.gov/pmc/articles/PMC2424090/.

8. Yasmin A. (2016, September 06). *White Racism Linked to Fatal Heart Disease for Blacks and Whites.* Berkley News. http://news.berkeley.edu/2016/09/06/racism-heart-health/.

9. Seppala, E. (2014, May 8). *Connectedness & Health: The Science of Social Connection.* The Center for Compassion and Altruism Research and Education. http://ccare.stanford.edu/uncategorized/connectedness-health-the-science-of-social-connection-infographic/.

10. Sue, D.W. (2011, February 27). *How Does Oppression (Microaggressions) Affect Perpetrators?* Psychology Today. https://www.psychology-today.com/us/blog/microaggressions-in-everyday-life/201102/how-does-oppression-microaggressions-affect.

11. Perry, S. (2008, November 16). *Mirror Neurons.* BrainFacts.org. http://www.brainfacts.org/archives/2008/mirror-neurons.

12. Walford, M. (2017, July 28). *Stress: It's Not in Your Head, it's in Your Nervous System.* UPLIFT. https://upliftconnect.com/stress-its-not-in-your-head-its-in-your-nervous-system/.

We Are All Connected

1. MacMillan, T. (2018, March 14). *The World is Smaller Than You Think.* New York Magazine. https://www.thecut.com/2018/03/the-history-of-the-six-degrees-of-separation-study.html.

2. Davidson, J. (2014, January 1). *News: Six-ish Degrees of Separation.* Psychology Today. https://www.psychologytoday.com/us/articles/201401/news-six-ish-degrees-separation.

3. Wolpert, S. (2019, May 10). *UCLA Neuroscientist's Book Explains Why Social Connection is as Important as Food and Shelter.* UCLA. https://newsroom.ucla.edu/releases/we-are-hard-wired-to-be-social-248746.

4. Harvard Health Publishing. (2017, June). *Can Relationships Boost Longevity and Well-Being?* https://www.health.harvard.edu/mental-health/can-relationships-boost-longevity-and-well-being#:~:text=Social%20connections%20appear%20to%20be,Waldinger

5. Plante, T. G. (2012, July 2). *Helping Others Offers Surprising Benefits.* Psychology Today. https://www.psychologytoday.com/blog/do-the-right-thing/201207/helping-others-offers-surprising-benefits-0.

6. Better Up. (2019, September 10). *The Value of Belonging at Work: New Frontiers for Inclusion.* https://get.betterup.co/rs/600-WTC-654/images/BetterUp_BelongingReport_091019.pdf.

7. Steinbuch, Y. (2017, November 17). *Apple's Diversity Chief Out After Outcry*. New York Post. https://nypost.com/2017/11/17/apples-diversity-chief-lasts-just-six-months/.

There Are Many Ways To Be Right

1. Britannica. (n.d.). *Physiology*. https://www.britannica.com/science/information-theory/Physiology.

2. Gustafson, C. (2017, December). *Bruce Lipton, PhD: The Jump From Cell Culture to Consciousness*. Integrative Medicine: A Clinician's Journal. https://www.ncbi.nlm.nih.gov/pmc/articles/PMC6438088/.

3. Urry, A. (2019, August 16). *Scientists Know Gravity Exists. They Just Don't Know How it Works*. The Washington Post. https://www.washingtonpost.com/outlook/scientists-know-gravity-exists-they-just-dont-know-how-it-works/2019/08/16/7ad9cfe6-9786-11e9-830a-21b9b36b64ad_story.html.

Having Conversations

1. MacMillan, T. (2018, March 14). *The Classic Study That Showed the World is Smaller Than You Think*. The Cut. https://www.thecut.com/2018/03/the-history-of-the-six-degrees-of-separation-study.html.

2. McCuistion, S. (2020). The Hidden Cost of Doing Business. In M. Mongan (Ed.), *Brilliant Breakthroughs for the Small Business Owner: Fresh Perspectives on Profitability, People, Productivity, and Finding Peace in Your Business* (pp.63-73). Brilliant Breakthroughs, Inc.

3. Forbes Communication Council. (2020, March 2). *12 Benefits of Embracing Vulnerability in Leadership*. Forbes. https://www.forbes.com/sites/forbescommunicationscouncil/2020/03/02/12-benefits-of-embracing-vulnerability-in-leadership/#3daef3962248.

A Win-Win Proposition

1. United States Department of Agriculture. (n.d.). *School Breakfast Program (SBP) Fact Sheet.* https://www.fns.usda.gov/sbp/fact-sheet.

2. Milkman, A. (2016, February 16). *The Radical Origins of Free Breakfast for Children.* Eater. https://www.eater.com/2016/2/16/11002842/free-breakfast-schools-black-panthers.

3. Milkman, A. (2016, February 16). *The Radical Origins of Free Breakfast for Children.* Eater. https://www.eater.com/2016/2/16/11002842/free-breakfast-schools-black-panthers.

4. United States Department of Agriculture. (n.d.). *School Breakfast Program History.* https://www.fns.usda.gov/sbp/program-history.

5. United States Equal Employment Opportunity Commission. (n.d.). *The Pregnancy Discrimination Act of 1978.* https://www.eeoc.gov/statutes/pregnancy-discrimination-act-1978.

6. McKinsey Global Institute. (2015, September 1). *How Advancing Women's Equality Can Add $12 Trillion to Global Worth.* McKinsey & Company. https://www.mckinsey.com/featured-insights/employment-and-growth/how-advancing-womens-equality-can-add-12-trillion-to-global-growth.

7. Hewlett, S.A., Marshall, M., & Sherbin, L. (2013, December). *How Diversity Can Drive Innovation.* Harvard Business Review. https://hbr.org/2013/12/how-diversity-can-drive-innovation.

8. Andrew, S. (2021, February 16). *Reparations for Slavery Could Have Reduced Covid-19 Transmission and Deaths in the US, Harvard Study Says.* CNN. https://www.cnn.com/2021/02/16/us/reparations-covid-black-americans-disparity-trnd/index.html?utm_medium=social&utm_source=fbCNN&utm_content=2021-02-17T06%3A00%3A36&utm_term=link.

9. Keltner, D. (2004, March 1). *The Compassionate Instinct.* Greater Good Magazine. https://greatergood.berkeley.edu/article/item/the_compassionate_instinct.

Becoming Aware

1. Thompson, P. (2017, January 16). *How Mindfulness Helped a Workplace Diversity Exercise.* Harvard Business Review. https://hbr.org/2017/01/how-mindfulness-helped-a-workplace-diversity-exercise.

Are You Who You Say You Are?

1. Hofstede, G., Hofstede, G. J., & Minkov, M. (2010). *Cultures and Organizations Software of the Mind: Intercultural Cooperation and its Importance for Survival.* (3rd ed., pp. 53-88). New York: McGraw-Hill.

2. Birkinshaw, J., & Cable, D. (2017, February 1). *The Dark Side of Transparency.* McKinsey & Company. https://www.mckinsey.com/business-functions/organization/our-insights/the-dark-side-of-transparency.

3. Hofstede, G., Hofstede, G. J., & Minkov, M. (2010). *Cultures and Organizations Software of the Mind: Intercultural Cooperation and its Importance for Survival.* (3rd ed., pp. 89-134). New York: McGraw-Hill.

The Strength of Vulnerability

1. Sime, C. (2019, March 27). *Could a Little Vulnerability Be the Key to Better Leadership?* Forbes. https://www.forbes.com/sites/carleysime/2019/03/27/could-a-little-vulnerability-be-the-key-to-better-leadership/.

2. Wallace, K. (2014, February 14). *What Your Baby Knows Might Freak You Out.* CNN. https://www.cnn.com/2014/02/13/living/what-babies-know-anderson-cooper-parents/index.html.

3. Project Implicit. (n.d.). http://implicit.harvard.edu/implicit/.

4. Chen, T. (2013, December 8). *21 Questions Asian People Are Sick of Answering.* BuzzFeed. https://www.buzzfeed.com/tanyachen/questions-asian-people-are-sick-of-answering?utm_term=.iqKMRMk4o#.ttJzaz72X.

5. *HeartMath® Certified Trainer: Leaders Guide,* HeartMath, Inc., Boulder Creek, CA, 2019.

6. Grabmeier, J. (2016, April 12). *The 6 Elements of an Effective Apology, According to Science*. The Ohio State University. https://news.osu.edu/ the-6-elements-of-an-effective-apology-according-to-science/.

Keeping an Open Mind

1. The Free Dictionary. (n.d.). *Feather*. https://www.thefreedictionary. com/feather.

2. Hopkin, M. (2007, April 30). *Seeing the Blues*. Nature. https:// www.nature.com/news/2007/070430/full/news070430-2. html#:~:text=Russian%20speakers%20divide%20what%20 the,and%20dark%20blue%20as%20distinct.

3. Phillips, K.W. (2014, October 01). *How Diversity Makes Us Smarter*. Scientific American. https://www.scientificamerican.com/article/ how-diversity-makes-us-smarter/.

Your Emotional Guidance System

1. Small, G., & Vorgan, G. (2011, February 18). *Is the Internet Killing Empathy?* CNN. https://edition.cnn.com/2011/OPINION/02/18/ small.vorgan.internet.empathy/#:~:text=Empathy%20is%20 learned%2C%20but%20it,%22internet%2Dna%C3%AFve%22%20 volunteers.

2. Internet World Stats. (n.d.). *Internet Users and 2020 Population in North America*. https://www.internetworldstats.com/stats14.htm.

3. Berliner, U. (2020, June 22). *Get a Comfortable Chair: Permanent Work from Home is Coming*. NPR. https://www.npr.org/2020/06/22/870029658/ get-a-comfortable-chair-permanent-work-from-home-is- coming#:~:text=According%20to%20Global%20Workplace%20 Analytics,year%20working%20remotely%20half%20time.

4. Wiedemann, C. (n.d.). *The Great Transformation? The Cultural Implica- tions of COVID-19*. Barrett Values Centre. https://www.valuescentre. com/resource-library/covid/.

5. Barthel, M. (2014, August 10). *Black Men Need More Education Than White Men to Get Jobs.* The Atlantic. https://www.theatlantic.com/education/archive/2014/08/black-men-need-more-education-to-get-the-same-jobs/375770/.

6. National Bureau of Economic Research. (2003, September). *Employers' Replies to Racial Names.* https://www.nber.org/digest/sep03/w9873.html.

7. Patten, E. (2016, July 1). *Racial, Gender Wage Gaps Persist in U.S. Despite Some Progress.* Pew Research Center. https://www.pewresearch.org/fact-tank/2016/07/01/racial-gender-wage-gaps-persist-in-u-s-despite-some-progress/.

8. *HeartMath® Certified Trainer: Leader's Guide,* HeartMath, Inc., Boulder Creek, CA 2019

9. HeartMath. (n.d.). *Quick Coherence® Technique.* https://www.heartmath.com/quick-coherence-technique/.

Chapter 11: Compassionate Diversity®

1. McCuistion, S. (2018). Five Ways to Bring Compassion into Your Organization. In M. Mongan (Ed.), *Brilliant Breakthroughs for the Small Business Owner: Fresh Perspectives on Profitability, People, Productivity, and Finding Peace in Your Business* (pp.73-85). Brilliant Breakthroughs, Inc.

2. The Center for Compassion and Altruism Research and Education. (2013, April). *Compassion and Business 2013: Panel 1 of 4.* http://ccare.stanford.edu/videos/compassion-and-business-conference-2013-2/.

3. Hamlett, C. (2019, March 11). *How Stress Affects Your Work Performance.* Houston Chronicle. http://smallbusiness.chron.com/stress-affects-work-performance-18040.html.

4. Seppälä, E. (2013, April 22). *The Unexpected Benefits of Compassion for Business.* Psychology Today. https://www.psychologytoday.com/blog/feeling-it/201304/the-unexpected-benefits-compassion-business.

5. Seppälä, E., & Cameron, K. (2015, December 1). *Proof That Positive Work Cultures Are More Productive.* Harvard Business Review. https://hbr.org/2015/12/proof-that-positive-work-cultures-are-more-productive.

6. Fryer, B. (2013, September 18). *The Rise of Compassionate Management (Finally).* Harvard Business Review. https://hbr.org/2013/09/the-rise-of-compassionate-management-finally.

7. Cutway, A. (2016, May 4). *Orlando Man Uses Lunch Break to Teach Homeless Woman to Read.* Orlando Sentinel. https://www.orlandosentinel.com/features/gone-viral/os-orlando-man-homeless-woman-read-20160503-story.html.

8. *HeartMath® Certified Trainer: Leaders Guide*, HeartMath, Inc., Boulder Creek, CA, 2019.

About the Author

Susan McCuistion is a cultural practitioner and creator of Compassionate Diversity®, which integrates concepts from the fields of intercultural competence, emotional intelligence, leadership, science, and more into powerful tools for change. Compassionate Diversity® uses three interrelated concepts—Comprehension, Connection, and Collaboration—to build resilience and inclusion in organizations and in our world.

Susan offers 25 years of human resources speaking, consulting, and facilitating experience, together with specialty skills in national culture and subculture and diversity best practices. In addition to providing intercultural competency coaching to C-suite and senior leaders, she has developed and facilitated enterprise-wide cultural competency training in North America, Asia, Europe, and Latin America.

Throughout her career, Susan has amassed a variety of credentials. She is certified in multiple cultural tools, such as Barrett Values Centre Culture Assessments and the Intercultural Development Inventory® (IDI), and she is a HeartMath® Certified Resilience Coach and Facilitator. She has presented at conferences and on webinars for The Conference Board and Human Capital Institute. Her quotes and insights have appeared in articles in The New York Times and for publications by the Society of Human Resources Management (SHRM).

Susan's visionary approach led to the development of an online conference, New Diversity Summit™, even before online conferences became a way of life. She is co-founder of the Diversity Thought Leader Community™, and a #1 International Bestselling Business Author. On her Compassionate Business Connections™ blog, she offers practical tips for creating a more inclusive, compassionate, and resilient workplace.

Susan holds an M.S. in Statistics from the University of Nevada, Las Vegas. She is a registered member of the Oneida Nation.

Connect with Susan:

Website: susanmccuistion.com
LinkedIn: https://www.linkedin.com/in/susanmccuistion/
Facebook: https://www.facebook.com/SusanMcCuistion/
Twitter: https://twitter.com/SusanMcCuistion
Author Profile: amazon.com/author/susanmccuistion

We Invite You to Post a Review of this Book on Amazon and Goodreads!

Made in the USA
Monee, IL
11 July 2021